D1144715

Chamonix–Mont Blanc

Chamonix–Mont Blanc 1927/Oskar Kokoschka

Chamonix–Mont Blanc
Robin G Collomb

Alpine guide 1

Constable London

Published by
Constable & Company Ltd
10 Orange Street   London WC2

© Copyright 1969 Robin G Collomb
First published 1969
SBN 09 456490 6

Guidebooks by the same author

Companion volume in this series
Zermatt and District

Selected Climbs in the Pennine Alps *two volumes*
Selected Climbs in the Bernese Alps
Graians West
Graians East
Maritime Alps

With Peter Crew
Selected Climbs in the Mont Blanc Range *two volumes*
Bregaglia West

With J O Talbot
Bernina Alps

Photographs and diagrammatic information
prepared by
Alpina Technica Services
John Cleare and Robin Collomb

Book and maps designed by
Graham Bishop

Printed in England by
Butler & Tanner Ltd
Frome and London

Contents

vii

Illustrations

Fuller descriptive captions appear under photographs and illustrations in the guidebook
Those in italics below are maps

Abbreviations

A., Ave. Avenue

Aig. Aiguille *sharp peak*

C.A.F. French Alpine Club

C.A.I. Italian Alpine Club

C.G.C. Compagnie des Guides de Chamonix

É.A.G.C. École d'Alpinisme des Guides de Chamonix

É.H.M. École de Haute Montagne

É.N.S.A. École Nationale de Ski et d'Alpinisme

h. hour(s)

km. kilometre(s)

km./h. kilometres per hour

m. metres

min. minutes

ml. miles

Mt. Mont *mountain*

P., Pl. Place *Square*

R.N. Route Nationale *main road*

S.C.S.M. Société Chamoniarde de Secours en Montagne

T.M.B. Tour du Mt. Blanc *walk*. Also used by railway company for Tramway du Mt. Blanc

MB1, MB2 These letters refer to volumes I and II of *Selected Climbs in the Mont Blanc Range*, a guidebook for mountaineers, to which reference is occasionally made in descriptions of walking routes

Acknowledgements

The source of illustrations used in the guidebook is as
follows:

Frontispiece, by permission of the Art Museum,
Karlsruhe.

Photographs on pages 12, 38–39, 100, 110, 111, 114,
115, 117, 120–121, 138, 150, 208–209 by permission
of the French National Tourist Office. The remainder
were drawn from the collections of John Cleare and
Robin Collomb, and all the photographic material
was prepared in the studios of John Cleare. The
co-operation of the French National Tourist Office is
gratefully acknowledged for providing the latest data
and statistics concerning tourist movement and
facilities in the Chamonix valley.

Introduction

Chamonix is the largest of the major Alpine resorts in Europe. In 1965 the resident population was 7800. The locality has the capacity to cater for more visitors than any other summer resort of this category in Europe. This does not mean that Chamonix is the most attractive holiday place in the Alps. A comparison of this sort is always a matter of taste or opinion. Yet among the galaxy of splendid resorts dotted across the Alps for nearly 800 km., Chamonix is probably the busiest and liveliest. In this sense the atmosphere is more like the Mediterranean seaboard. Much of the recent increase in interest is due to the new road tunnel under Mt. Blanc, linking Chamonix and Courmayeur. This shortens the road journey between Paris and Milan, for instance, by 200 km.

Standing at the foot of Mt. Blanc, the highest mountain in Europe, the attraction of Chamonix speaks for itself. The Alps are the most densely populated range of mountains in the world, and the scenery is in a classic mould with which all other mountains are compared. Moreover, situated in Western Europe, with its highly developed system of communications, they are completely accessible. While the frontier between France and Italy is marked by the backbone of the Mt. Blanc range, Chamonix retains a character that is wholly French.

The pre-eminence of this great mountain accounts for the early popularity and rapid development of the Chamonix valley as a travellers' paradise. Some indication of the growth of interest is provided by statistics. In 1783 about 1500 visitors journeyed to the valley; in 1830 the number was 3000. It rose to 12,000 in 1865, at the peak of the 'Golden Age' of Alpine exploration. When the electric railway was opened at the turn of the century the number of visitors immediately before the First World War was 200,000. By 1938 this had swollen to 500,000. The figure today is put at one and a quarter million.

Chamonix has expanded out of all proportion to the progress made by a number of equally celebrated resorts. Obviously, the moderate altitude above sea level (about 1000 m.) and ease of access to its deep broad valley have contributed to this expansion. The valley is so deep that the summit of Mt. Blanc rises 3800 m. above the resort. This is the greatest vertical interval between a resort and its principal peak in the

Alps. More than anything, Chamonix owes its prosperity to the patronage of famous artists, writers, poets, philosophers, politicians, mountaineers and others, who flocked there during the 19th century. In those days it was a journey of three or four days from Paris and you arrived weary and bruised from horseback on a rough path beside the River Arve.

The traditional simplicity of life in an Alpine valley is found no more. Indeed it is doubtful whether this valley could be described as 'secluded' at any time during the present century. Chamonix is a metropolis for the area, with diversions and entertainments equal to those of a capital city.

Outwardly a great deal has changed, even in the past 20 years. Yet the scenery remains unchanged and unchangeable, and the enthusiasm to enjoy it is greater than ever. The visitor today has a wider choice of activities and more opportunity to enjoy them than his predecessor.

The valley is open all year round. The winter sports season is hardly finished when the 'summer' season begins. In April, this is much earlier than usual. A network of rack-and-pinion railways, cable cars, chair- and ski-lifts reaches up from the floor of the valley and carries sightseers high over the forests to moraines and glaciers of the peaks. Previously most of these could only be reached by the fittest walkers and climbers. This mountain transport system is the most elaborate in the Alps and in the world.

As a centre for skiing, Chamonix is not the most popular; the *pistes* are fairly steep and some of the best ski-runs are rather difficult. So in winter the valley tends to attract the more experienced performer.

The double-barrelled name of *Chamonix–Mt. Blanc* was officially adopted by the community as long ago as 1922. Since then most of the inhabitants (Chamoniards) have been engaged in the tourist industry, so that husbandry has become less important to the economy of the district. Light engineering and other commercial enterprises have grown up in the town, and further diversification of industry will result from benefits afforded by the presence of the tunnel.

The holidaymaker today is essentially a mobile visitor with international aspirations. He is able to move quickly and cheaply from place to place if his interest lags. Chamonix is such a wide area, with unlimited possibilities for touring by rail, coach or car, that it makes an ideal base. One also to which it is always a pleasure to return. Uniquely, it even has a helicopter service; passengers are flown high into the mountains in a matter of minutes. Switzerland is a short road or rail journey to the head of the valley, and Italy is at the other end of the tunnel, 20 km. away.

A favourite observation of writers in the past, who invariably did not care for towns and social life, was that a few minutes suffice to see Chamonix but it would take months to see its surroundings. No town in the world lies in the centre of such a glorious crown of granite spires, glaciers and snowy peaks. This guidebook attempts to describe these imposing surroundings for the benefit of all kinds of visitors—for those who have two days or two or three weeks to spend in the neighbourhood—for those whose aims do not rise above simple pedestrian excursions—to those who wish to climb the rocks and ice of the heights.

The reader is asked to forgive the writer for confining most of his remarks to practical indications for the amenities and excursions described. Eloquent descriptions of scenery and experience in the district can be found in a variety of personal accounts published over the years.

Robin G Collomb
Goring on Thames
December, 1968

Chamonix—some preliminary information

Origins—A Benedictine convent, founded in 1091, established the first communal centre, thereafter known as *Le Prieuré*. This name persisted till the valley was discovered by the outside world. The inhabitants, farmers and hunters, were ruled by the authority of the priory and were freed from its yoke on the eve of the French Revolution.

Discovery—In the tourist sense, by the Englishmen William Windham and Pococke in 1741, whose curiosity was roused from the shores of Lake Geneva by the distant gleaming snows of Mt. Blanc. The tale of this journey reached the drawing rooms of Geneva and London, and others followed suit.

Name—*Chamouni* was the native description of the valley (Lat. *Campus munitus*, sheltered by the mountains). The visit of Windham and Pococke inspired its adoption as the name for the chief settlement.

Mt. Blanc—First climbed by Jacques Balmat and Dr. Michel-Gabriel Paccard on 8 August, 1786. Both men were natives of Chamonix. Balmat was 25, some 5 ft. 3 in. tall and a crystal and chamois hunter; Paccard was 30 and the village doctor. Their ascent caused some consternation and disbelief among rivals for the prize, and the climb was soon repeated. First ascent by an Englishman: Mark Beaufoy, 3 August, 1787. By an American: Dr. J. van Rensselaer, 1819. By a woman: the Chamonix maid-servant, Marie Paradis, in 1809.

Valley—The River Arve flows in the bottom. The main part, broad and fairly flat, is 15 km. long and extends from the village of Les Houches (1007 m.) at the lower end to Argentière (1252 m.) at the upper. The entrance is from Le Fayet (591 m.), through a narrow rocky defile. In the middle, Chamonix (1040 m.) stands in the broadest part and the main road has a bypass to the south, from which a spur branches into the Mt. Blanc Tunnel. For administrative purposes Chamonix embraces most of the valley as a commune. The population of the conurbation is about 7800.

Electric Railway—From Le Fayet to Chamonix, 19 km., opened in 1901. Chamonix–Argentière to Vallorcine at Swiss frontier, 15 km. The railway continues to Martigny in Switzerland, $21\frac{1}{2}$ km., where it joins the international rail route through the Rhone valley.

Montenvers Railway—Opened in 1908. Rack-and-pinion permanent way from Chamonix to the Mer de Glace, 5 km., 1 in $2\frac{1}{2}$ gradient.

Mont Blanc Tunnel—Opened in 1965, the longest road tunnel in the world. Entrance above Les Pèlerins to south of town. It is 11·6 km. long, passes 2480 m. under the mountain and emerges near the hamlet of Entrèves in Italy, from where the new main road bypasses the resort of Courmayeur. Two single illuminated carriageways, air-conditioned, speed limit of 70 km./h. The tunnel is provided with narrow pedestrian sidewalks, used in emergency only. Normal driving time, 15–20 min.; on foot, 3 h. Toll charges.

Mer de Glace—This is the longest glacier in the district, 14 km. from its source, and the fourth longest in the Alps. The lower reaches, about 700 m. wide, are bare ice—hence the name—and the tongue descends to within 500 m. of the valley floor. On either side the Bossons and Argentière glaciers glide down to within 300 m. of the valley.

Aiguilles—The name given generally to the collection of remarkable granite spires which directly overlook the town. In modern times these rust-brown pinnacles have proved to be more of an attraction than any other feature of the valley. The highest of them, the Aiguille du Midi (3842 m.), is reached by a cableway. This is the highest *téléphérique* in the Alps and it continues in an aerial situation above the glaciers, right across the Mt. Blanc range, to Courmayeur.

How to get there

From all points in Northern France, from Britain and the United States, the first destination is Paris.

From the Low Countries, Germany and Scandinavia it is usually necessary to reach Basel or Zurich and cross Switzerland.

From the south of France the first destination is Lyon. From northern Italy you start from Turin.

These are overland approaches by rail and are served by fast trains with first- and second-class seats and sleeping cars.

Road routes are approximately the same as rail.

For air routes, the nearest international airport to Chamonix is Geneva (Cointrin). There is a through carriage rail service from Geneva to Chamonix in $2\frac{1}{2}$ h.

From Paris

Express trains with through carriages from Lyon Station in Paris run to Chamonix about five times a day. The journey takes 10 h. The route is by Dijon, Mâcon, Bourg, Culoz, Aix-les-Bains, Annecy, La Roche (junction with route from Geneva) and *Le Fayet*. From here the last stage up the valley takes 35 min.

From Basel or Zurich

By train to Lausanne or Geneva. From Lausanne another train is taken to Martigny, where you join the mountain railway crossing the Col des Montets via Châtelard and Vallorcine to Chamonix. This journey is less complicated than it appears. The time taken will depend on connections; on average about 6 h. from Basel or Zurich to Chamonix.

From Geneva join the service mentioned in the General section above (also from Paris).

From Lyon

The Paris route is joined at Culoz and the journey to Chamonix takes 4 h.

From Turin

Frequent rail and express coach services follow the Aosta valley by Ivrea, Châtillon and Aosta to the railhead at Pré St. Didier, 5 km. from Courmayeur. From there you go by road through the Mt. Blanc tunnel to Chamonix, reached in some $2\frac{1}{2}$ h. from Turin.

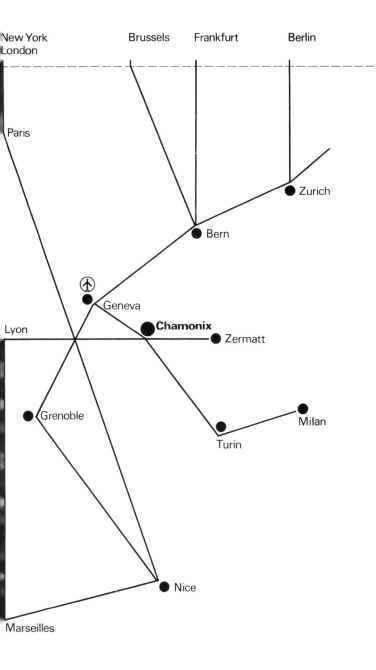

Approach routes to Chamonix

Zermatt to Chamonix connecting service

This rail journey is done frequently by visitors moving from the Swiss resort of Zermatt to Chamonix, and vice versa. The route is: Zermatt–Visp/Brig–Martigny–Chamonix. There is an excellent service on both mountain railway sections of the route (up to 10 trains a day), and the fast section between Brig and Martigny in the Rhone valley is covered in 1 h. With good connections the average time occupied in travelling between the resorts is 5 h.

Rail services to Chamonix

From	ml.	km.	Journey time (h.)	Change at
Paris	450	725	10	
Geneva	60	100	$2\frac{1}{2}$	sometimes La Roche
Basel	175	280	6	Lausanne/Martigny or Geneva
Zurich	190	300	6	as above
Lyon	170	275	4	Culoz or Aix-les-Bains
Turin	100	160	$3\frac{1}{2}$	Pré St. Didier
Zermatt	85	130	5	Visp/Brig and Martigny
London to Paris	290	470	8	

All these starting points except Zermatt can be reached by air.

Fares

The stability of fares is too uncertain for a schedule to have much value except for the current year. For a simple illustration, in 1968 the second-class return rail fare with tourist reduction, valid for one month, from London to Chamonix was £22 (sleeper extra). Comparable fare by flying to Geneva, then by train, £40.

Europabus

An international consortium of long-haul coach companies, controlled by 16 European railway administrations, operates a network service between large cities; notably from Amsterdam, Brussels, Paris, Geneva, Innsbruck, Milan, Turin, Venice and Nice. Many of these services reach or cross the Alps. Travelling in a fast modern coach is comfortable and there are good opportunities for the more leisurely study of scenery. Fares are appreciably less than rail.

Services of particular interest for reaching Chamonix are those from Nice, twice daily; from Geneva, four times a day; from Turin, four or five times; from Milan, once a day.

Local time
Arriving from Italy, care should be taken to note whether Italian local time is the same as in France (Chamonix). In 1968 Italy was one hour ahead for summer time than the rest of Western Europe.

*Part of the Mt. Blanc range from Sallanches. Mt. Blanc in centre,
Aig. du Midi on left, Dômes de Miage on right*

Mer de Glace

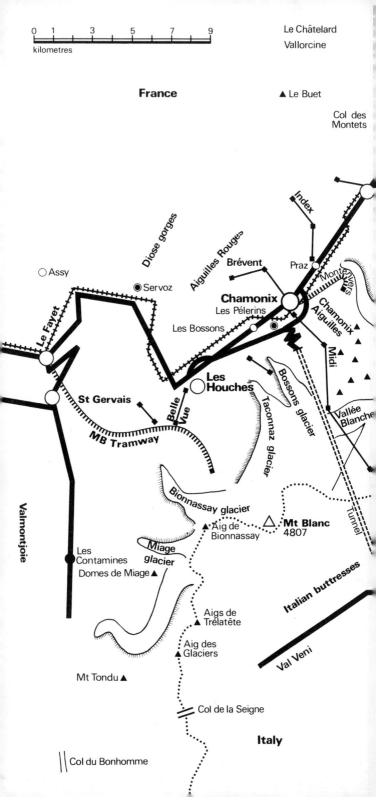

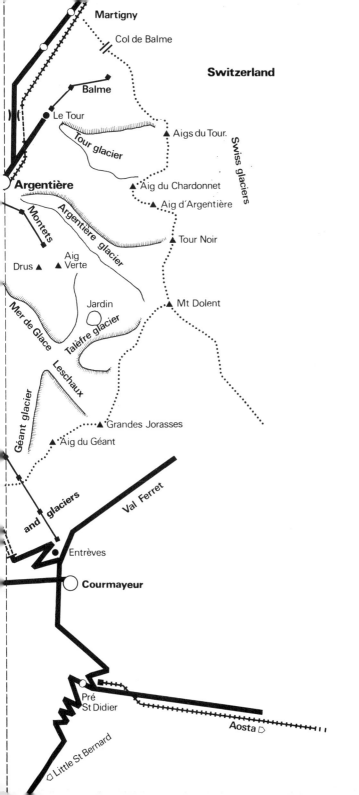

Into the Chamonix valley

Le Fayet is an industrial centre below the fine resort of *St. Gervais-les-Bains* (800 m.). This pleasant town clings haphazardly to a sloping shelf above a narrow gorge in the entrance to the adjoining Montjoie valley. St. Gervais has rather grand buildings, as befits a spa, and is noted for its thermal baths (sulphur). The resort has a separate and more exclusive clientele than Chamonix. In this pretty spot there is no way out at the head of Val Montjoie for motor vehicles. This is the starting point for climbing Mt. Blanc by what is traditionally called the 'St. Gervais Route'. In fact this approach to the mountain can be used with equal convenience from the Chamonix valley; from there it is the preferred route to the summit for the majority who contemplate the ascent.

The *Mt. Blanc Tramway*, a modern narrow-gauge rack-and-pinion railway, climbs from Le Fayet–St. Gervais in wide curves to rocky slopes on the St. Gervais Route near the Bionnassay glacier. Views into the Valmontjoie are very beautiful and the tramway crosses broad open pastures on the Col de Voze. This is a walker's paradise with terrific views across the north side of the Mt. Blanc range. In winter these slopes provide a number of easy ski-runs, and many ski-tows are brought into use.

The military airfield at Le Fayet is restricted to certain types of aircraft and helicopters, and the Air Mountain Rescue Service for the region is based here. Light aircraft can be hired for short flights into the mountain range.

From Le Fayet the railway and road more or less follow a parallel course into the Chamonix valley. The road was constructed by Napoleon III, on the left bank of the river; on the other side the old road winds high above the gorge of the Arve. At the foot of the gorge is an industrial complex at Chedde. Much higher, well above the old road, you can visit the hamlet of *Assy* (994 m.) on a sunny plateau (bus service). Here you find the chapel of Notre-Dame-de-Toute-Grâce, completed in 1950. It is quite unique, being virtually a museum of 20th-century French art. Novarina supervised the harmonious design and commissioned the interior decorations. Included are works by Léger (mosaics), Strawinsky (mosaics), Braque (painting of tabernacle), Chagall (font), Lipchitz (statue), Bonnard (painting, one of his last works), Lurçat (tapestry), Derain (tableau), and Rouault, Bazaine, Berçat, Brianchon, Bony and Huré (stained-glass windows). The locality has good hotels and pensions and a variety of charming walks revealing lakes and waterfalls and an extensive view of Mt. Blanc to the south.

After passing the smelting works at Chedde (products for explosives, 'cheddite'), the constricted opening to the valley is reached. The road joins the railway at a bend; they run together through a wooded depression separated from the gorge by a low ridge. Crossing a small glade and emerging from a tunnel, the village of Servoz is seen, where the old road joins the valley. Behind Servoz is the famous and now commercialised beauty spot of the *Diose* (*Diosaz*) *gorge* (admission fee). An electricity generating station is passed and the river is crossed by an impressively high viaduct. The darkly furrowed mass of the Aig. du Goûter, overtopped by the snowy cap of the Dôme du Goûter, rise into view. These are high steps on the ridge to Mt. Blanc, whose summit is concealed.

From this point you look along the whole length of the Chamonix valley, a long straight trench which at first sight reveals few of its famous landmarks. The lower ends of rubble-strewn glaciers streaming towards the valley condescend to show themselves between their thickly wooded spurs; but little else. Seeing the mountain range sideways-on, from the great depths of the valley, the splendid scenery of the heights is mainly hidden.

The new autobahn-type road leading to the Mt. Blanc tunnel has replaced the old carriageway. This forks left and somewhat inconspicuously from the new motorway a short distance from Les Bossons. The old road and railway continue near the river while the new road swings above the valley to bypass the conurbation and enter the town near the railway station. A spur from this road climbs in zigzags to the tunnel.

There is a railway halt for Servoz and another for *Les Houches* (1007 m.). The latter village is scattered across a green hillside some distance above both roads and the river. Les Houches is perhaps the most peaceful holiday place in this bustling valley. Most of the houses have been rebuilt since the last war; there are many fine villas and ample accommodation for visitors can be found in a quiet setting. Flowered fields

17

and geranium boxes displayed everywhere make this village particularly inviting.

The *Bellevue cableway* starts at Les Houches and rises to the Col de Voze where the Mt. Blanc tramway can be joined. (Coming from Chamonix it is better to take a local bus to Les Houches, to avoid a walk of one km. from the railway station.)

At *Les Bossons* you can see the Simond factory where mountaineering equipment is made. On the right the sharp tentacle of the Bossons glacier feels its way towards the bed of the valley. Further along the old road and railway you pass a wooded picnic ground with small lakes on either side, and climbers' practice rocks are clearly visible through the trees. With so many gaily decorated houses clustered thickly on either side, the impression given is that you are coming into a much larger place than could have been believed. The road goes through the centre but the station is located on the east side of the town. The Montenvers station adjoins it and the motorway crosses both sets of tracks just outside the stations.

Looking back down the valley, Mt. Blanc, the Bosses ridge and the St. Gervais Route crowd the skyline and form a memorable backdrop to the scene (see frontispiece of Kokoschka's painting).

Summary

By rail from Le Fayet, 19 km., 35 min. journey time. By road from Le Fayet, classified R.N. No. 506 (called the Route Blanche), 19 km., 30–45 min. by car. You must use slip roads or laybys for stopping on this road to admire the scenery.

Local bus service from Le Fayet to Chamonix, calling at villages on slip roads either side of the main road.

The most frequent bus service (Cars Navettes) operates within the confines of the valley (i.e. not down to Le Fayet) and calls at all mountain cableways: Les Houches–Chamonix–Argentière–Le Tour. Hourly service between 08.00 and 19.30 h.

Historical note

Originally a Celtic tribe occupied the Chamonix valley and these people were overrun by the expanding Roman empire. An inscription found on the Col de la Forclaz, dated the year 74, is the earliest record of life in the valley. The act for founding a Benedictine priory in the valley bears the seal of Count Aymo of Geneva. A reference to Pope Urban II fixes the date about 1091. This deed conferred a grant of the Vale of Chamonix from the Col de Balme at its upper end to the stream coming from the Diose gorge near Servoz. The deed was published, together with an interesting collection of documents relating to the Priory, in the second half of the 19th century.

The first recorded visit of the Bishop of Geneva, within whose diocese Chamonix lay, was in 1443. His journey began in the summer. After a sojourn with the Abbot of Sallanches, he continued his arduous trek accompanied by the Abbot, his two officiating clerical attendants and some menials, all on foot, and the party did not arrive in Chamonix until 4 October.

In 1669 a treasury official named Le Pays wrote from 'Chamony, en Fossigny' to a lady of his acquaintance the first description we have of the mountains of Chamonix. 'Here, Madame, I see five mountains which are just like you—five mountains which are pure ice from top to bottom.' Obviously he was referring to the five glacier tongues which descend towards the valley. (The reader must guess which way his simile is supposed to be taken!)

The Chamoniards were independent and rebellious by nature, and many of them were dedicated to smuggling goods across the passes to Italy. Arms and contraband were even stored in the priory. It can be assumed that this was permitted by the prior in order to win allegiance from the natives and persuade them to pay their taxes. From the time (1530) that permission was granted to the priory by Philip of Savoy, Count of Geneva, for the inhabitants to hold a weekly fair, the valley had long had intercourse and trade with neighbours. These fairs, held at the priory, brought many strangers. Nothing however was known of the scenery of Mt. Blanc. Even at Geneva, a seat of learning and intellectual pursuits, it was a matter of dispute whether the great snowy masses of 'Les Glacières' seen on the horizon lay north or south of the valley. On some maps they were even placed to the west.

It was a young Englishman, William Windham, about 23 years old, and his tutor, Dr. Pococke, who, with several friends, came to Chamonix in 1741 and gave a report to the Royal Society that drew general attention to the sublime scenery. This account served the purpose though it painted a gloomy and terrifying picture of the mountains. A stone where the party is supposed to have slept at the side of the Mer de Glace was called Pierre des Anglais. Having been broken by a shepherd's fire, another was placed there with an inscription—thus falsifying the 'evidence' and committing the first act in the name of tourism.

Following the visit of Pierre Martel, a Genevese instrument maker, he published a description of the mountains which were termed 'Ice-Alps'. This emphasised the popular opinion that the glaciers were solid ice mountains.

These early illusions about the horrors of the journey and the dreaded surroundings were swept away by the noted Genevese scientist and geologist, Horace Bénédict de Saussure, who first visited Chamonix in 1760. A few years later he was followed by his fellow townsman, Marc-Théodore Bourrit, an artist and precentor of Geneva cathedral. From the start they set their sights on climbing Mt. Blanc. In fact de Saussure made the second ascent. The modern invasion had begun.

After 696 years of government by a prior, the commune of Chamonix purchased its freedom from the priory taxes in 1786 for the sum of 58,000 livres. The Chamoniards are said to have bitterly regretted their bargain when the French revolution broke out a few years later, as that would have relieved them from the bondage of the priory without any payment whatever.

From the day in 1855 when a great part of the village was burnt it lost its pristine simplicity for ever. Situated in the department of Haute-Savoie, Chamonix became a part of France in 1860 when it was ceded to the Emperor Napoleon by Victor Emmanuel as part of the price of French support in the struggle for unification. For a long time after it enjoyed freedom for travellers entering from Switzerland to pass customs without any examination of luggage.

In their turn a host of famous men and women visited Chamonix in the late 18th and 19th centuries—Goethe, Chateaubriand, Victor Hugo, Ruskin, Alexandre Dumas, George Sand, Napoleon III, Pasteur, Théophile Gautier, Byron, Shelley, etc. None of these savants actually climbed Mt. Blanc. Later celebrities are too numerous to mention, but this interest in Chamonix and its scenery outweighs anything shown in other resorts at least tenfold. Several films for cinema have been made in the valley, the most notable perhaps being *The Mountain*, with the late Spencer Tracy. A television spectacular was filmed in a blizzard on the Aig. du Midi about 10 years ago, which included the British mountaineer Joe Brown, and was relayed on Eurovision.

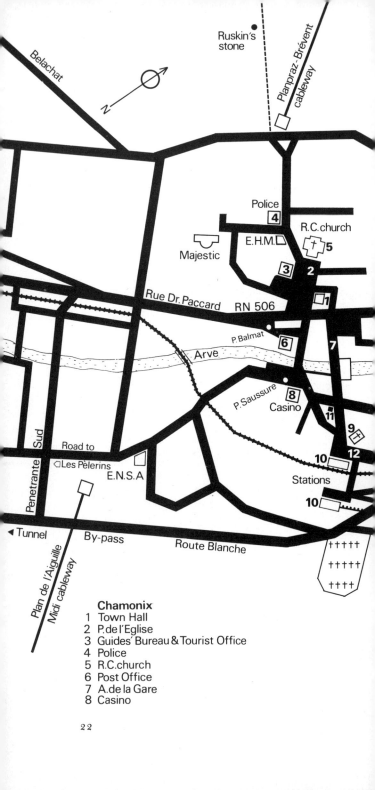

Ruskin's
stone

Belachat

Planpraz-Brévent cableway

Police
4

R.C.church

E.H.M.

5 ✝

Majestic

3

2

Rue Dr. Paccard   RN 506

1

P.Balmat

6

Arve

7

P.Saussure

8

Casino

11

9

Road to

◁Les Pèlerins

E.N.S.A

12

10

Stations

Penetrante Sud

10

◀ Tunnel   By-pass   Route Blanche

✝✝✝✝✝
✝✝✝✝✝
✝✝✝✝

Plan de l'Aiguille Midi cableway

Chamonix
1 Town Hall
2 P.de l'Eglise
3 Guides' Bureau & Tourist Office
4 Police
5 R.C.church
6 Post Office
7 A.de la Gare
8 Casino

22

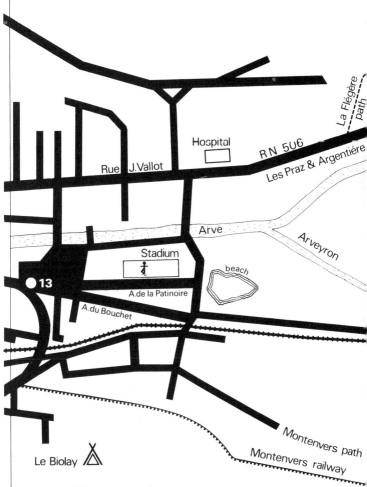

0 — 500 metres

Hospital

La Flégère path

RN 506

Rue J.Vallot

Les Praz & Argentiére

Arve

Arveyron

Stadium

beach

13

A.de la Patinoire

A.du Bouchet

Montenvers path

Montenvers railway

Le Biolay

9 English chapel
10 Stations
11 C.A.F (French Alpine Club)
12 P.de la Gare
13 P.du Mont Blanc
     E.H.M (Mountaineering School)
     E.N.S.A (National School for
     Skiing and Mountaineering)

The town

Chamonix is generally regarded as unlovely, for it does not bear comparison with many smaller and prettier Alpine resorts. As a town, however, it has much more to offer because it is so large. Indeed the physical changes in size and layout have completely transformed the resort compared with only 20 years ago. Even the residents complain that they are confused by the 'work in progress' which extends to new roads and buildings that seemingly appear overnight in a continual process at present. (For instance, there is practically no open ground on either side of the road, itself greatly improved, between the town centre and Les Pèlerins.) Cranes overtopping the changing skyline of new buildings and contractors' lorries are already a familiar part of the scene. The population of the main centre is now reckoned as 8500, although this figure is in excess of the total for the entire commune as counted at the last census. The local authority has introduced new regulations for residence and it is probably more difficult for a foreigner to set up home in Chamonix than in almost any comparable resort. While the language is French a good deal of English and Italian is spoken, and a little German.

It is true to say that every day in Chamonix is reminiscent of an English Bank Holiday. You walk shoulder to shoulder with crowds along the pavements. Cars cruising in the streets, looking for niches in which to park, would prove a nightmare even to the seasoned police forces of London and New York. The boulevard atmosphere so typical of France is very much in evidence and the only sure way of resting your feet is to find an unoccupied chair in a café-bar on the sidewalk.

Buses start from the station and the Place du Mt. Blanc. *Shopping facilities* are excellent and all kinds of goods and services that you would expect to find only in a large city are available. A table showing the number and location of public services is given at the end of this section.

A large central *carpark* is located in the Place du Mt. Blanc; also in all the central squares (places), though finding a space is a matter of luck. More reliable parking can be found beside the bypass road where it swings across the tracks of both railways. There is limited parking at the station: *taxi rank*. The lower stations of all cableways encircling the town have carparks. Facing you outside the main station is the Avenue de la Gare, leading to the hub where the *tourist inquiry office* and *post office* are found in the Place de l'Église (400 m.).

Something like 50 *hotels* of all prices and categories are crowded into the town. There are officially 97 recognised for the valley, which have been inspected by the Government Tourist Office. This excludes St. Gervais, which is treated separately. These hotels provide 3500 beds and a further 1300 are available in a wide range of *furnished accommodation* for rent, and in cheap *chalet-dormitories*. Additionally there are many private holiday centres owned by social, commercial and sporting organisations. An interesting innovation is that all hotels issue *meal vouchers* which can be used at any other hotel or restaurant in the valley, including those in the mountains.

The *Youth Hostel* is situated at Les Pèlerins, 2·5 km. from the centre. A booking made many months in advance is necessary to secure a place.

For many years there was no official *campsite* at Chamonix. Broadly speaking this is still the situation. Since the end of the second war, camping holidays have boomed, and with little organisation or control this has tended to swamp the valley. Many campers use a site at the Biollay, behind the Montenvers railway station; it is closest to the main shopping centre. This site is always crowded, even though it has now been removed to the adjoining woods behind the Refuge des Amis on the footpath to the Blaitière chalets. There is no running water or toilet facilities. The best campsites tend to lie beyond the outskirts of the town. There is an excellent one at Les Pèlerins, only a short distance above the river (signpost on old main road), with good facilities; and another at Les Bossons, near the chairlift. The authorities try to encourage campers to make inquiries at the tourist office, which has a list of 22 private sites round the town.

In the immediate vicinity you can go *horse riding* beside the river at Les Praz, about 1·5 km. along the Argentière road. Here also is a 9-hole *golf course*, due to be extended to 18 holes. Lessons and competitions are held. A mini golf course can be found at the other end of town near Les Pèlerins. *Bathers* have a beach at the Lac du Bouchet (diving board, etc., restaurant) in a pretty woodland setting north of the station. On the west side of the lake are public *tennis courts* with good facilities (showers, etc.), and there are other courts at the Majestic conference centre, open to the public. Several hotels have private courts. Also close to the Bouchet playground is the huge Olympic *ice rink* and *stadium*, built for the 8th Games in 1924, and subsequently enlarged and improved. Ice skating is possible throughout the summer with weekly competitions and skating performances (seats for 2000). *Bowling* is played at the Chamois cabaret club beside the bridge over the river at the bottom of the Avenue de la Gare. At the Aiguille du Midi cableway station an artificial *ski jump* is used for entertainment during summer. At Les Bossons a ski jump of Olympic proportions is closed in summer. *Angling* is possible in the river and one or two small lakes—fly fishing for trout. Permission is required and information should be sought from the tourist office.

Amusements are led by the new *Casino* where games are played daily from 15.00; Roulette, Baccara, Boule and Chemin de Fer; dancing and dinner in the evening. The town has four *cinemas*, seven *cabarets* and half a dozen *dance floors* in hotels and bars. Something resembling a *zoo* is an enclosure of mountain animals at the Montenvers Hotel. Children will appreciate the well-intentioned description: 'Garden of Fur-bearing Animals'.

Chamonix is somewhat deficient in cultural attractions, a fault it shares with nearly all other Alpine resorts. There is no museum, although the permanent exhibition of *Gabriel-Loppé*'s work is recommended to those with an interest in painting. The large gallery is the former studio of the artist and 60 canvases are on display. In the second half of the 19th century the artist climbed with such famous alpinists as Edward Whymper, Sir Leslie Stephen (who called him 'the court painter of Mt. Blanc') and Achille Ratti (Pope Pius XI). The gallery is reached through a passage between two shops on the Avenue de la Gare.

Of course the major attraction of the town is window-shopping. For the specialist, some of the best mountaineering equipment in the world can be bought here; Snell Sports in the Rue Dr. Paccard is known internationally. Walking through the town, in the Place de Saussure no one can fail to notice the statue of de Saussure and Balmat, facing Mt. Blanc, the latter anxiously pointing the way to the summit. Across the river, the Catholic church is not of special interest and you pass it to reach the Brévent cableway station.

A fascinating pastime for all strollers in Alpine resorts is a visit to the *cemetery*. Chamonix has three, but the one of special interest is that in which the small English church stands. This is opposite the railway station, and it is now almost hidden by new buildings. This cemetery comes fully up to expectations—if you know the stories behind simple inscriptions and, in some cases, how the buried came to be there at all. Here lies Edward Whymper (1840–1911), conqueror of the Matterhorn and simultaneously victim for the rest of his life of the greatest emotional disaster in the history of mountaineering. Refusing all aid and medical attention he died alone in a Chamonix hotel bedroom. Macabre stories belong to those who were victims of early accidents on Mt. Blanc. Capt. Henry Arkwright is interred below a simple headstone. In 1866 he and his guides were overwhelmed by falling ice while climbing the mountain. Bodies of the dead guides were recovered but no trace was found of the English captain. Thirty-one years later his dismembered remains together with articles of clothing and equipment—all perfectly preserved as new—were released near the bottom of the Bossons glacier. This was no less than 7 km. further down and nearly 3000 m. lower in height from the point where the party had been engulfed. Other accidents and similar circumstances affecting the long recovery of mutilated bodies have occurred on the mountain. Over the years, when the glaciers have disgorged their more gruesome secrets, attempts to put the objects recovered on public display have been banned.

On a brighter note the breezy movement of life and people in Chamonix is due to the holiday population continually shifting its attention and interest. Somehow this does not suit the character of the town, which is basically old-fashioned. On either side of the valley cableways zooming up to the showpieces of the Brévent and Aig. du Midi cream off hundreds daily. Most if not all of them return in the late afternoon and are swallowed up by hotels, bars, night clubs and cinemas. From the town the mountain views are not outstanding. Even if you dislike walking there is such a tremendous array of 'mechanical mountaineers' to choose from that everyone—at some expense—can travel upwards at many metres per second to some giddy height and feast on the majestic ice world.

Cableways

The Montenvers train is an ordinary journey in a railway carriage. Cableways are swifter, sensational and the journey too short to be uncomfortable. The longer lifts are generally in two stages. If you go only halfway up the journey is much cheaper. On the other hand you usually see much less by not going to the top station. A lot depends on whether you are making the trip for a breathtaking view and a lazy day in the restaurant, or with some walking excursion in mind. For the latter it is usual to travel on the first stage only; in most cases, from an upper station you have to be an experienced mountaineer or skier to venture off on foot.

Cableways fall into several categories. The largest variety, called a *téléphérique*, is an enclosed cabin in which up to 60 persons can travel by standing, although there are usually a few seats. A journey rarely takes more than 10 min. These cabins ride the fixed cable at speeds up to 30 km./h. in a plane inclined up to 45° from the horizontal. A smaller version is distinguished by the size of the cabin and is called *télécabine*. These carry from 4 to 20 persons and are usually the basis of the engineering system on upper stages. Another category of lift—certainly the most pleasant and refreshing to travel on—is the *télésiège*. It comprises a pair, or two pairs, of chairs, back to back, with a safety bar across the front in case you feel like falling out. A canvas awning can be unfurled over your head to keep off the sun or, if you are unlucky, rain. These chairs ride along the fixed cable at frequent intervals and the distance you are carried above the ground is much less than a téléphérique system. The smallest type of cableway is the *téléski* or skilift, which generally operates in winter, but there are several permanent fixtures at the appropriate altitude due to the recent development of summer skiing. This lift can be used at the head of téléphérique systems in summer if there are suitable nearby snowfields. In winter the portable nature of certain skilifts enables them to be placed where the snow is good for skiing. These lifts are usually called skitows. They consist of a tow-bar or umbrella hook, to which you either cling or lean back in and are pulled uphill at ground level, wearing your skis.

All these systems are in operation round Chamonix in summer and winter. Collectively they represent the most comprehensive network of mountain lifts in the world. Some of them are astonishing engineering feats and they are remarkably safe, although the highest cableways are closed in storm or winds that would not be regarded as dangerous to transport on level ground.

A table showing all cableways in the valley appears at the end of this section. Each one is described more fully in the excursions section.

Mountaineering services

The Mt. Blanc range is unsurpassed for mountaineering interest. The rock is mainly firm granite, a delight to handle, and the snow and ice climbing provide the widest possible variety of sport in all degrees of difficulty.

In Chamonix the company of registered guides (C.G.G.), founded in 1821, numbers some 150, of whom about 40 are full-time. Seventy years ago there were nearly three times this number climbing full-time in the valley. Since then two world wars, economic recessions and higher taxation have virtually eliminated the wealthy amateur alpinist who had six or eight weeks to spend each year in the mountains. High yet realistic charges for guided mountain tours and climbs coupled with the growth of guideless climbing among skilled amateurs have reduced the amount of work that professionals can obtain. Today the emphasis is put on climbing in fairly large groups, called 'collectives', where up to 10 or 12 persons can share two guides and climb mountains by their ordinary routes quite cheaply.

The *Guides' Bureau* is situated next door to the tourist inquiry office in the Place de l'Église. The bureau runs a *climbing school* (É.H.M. and É.A.G.C.) at favourable rates. Anyone wishing to try mountaineering during a holiday in the valley is strongly recommended to apply for one of the weekly courses. The traditional *Festival of Guides*, a parade in the streets, speeches, etc., takes place each year on 15 August.

The *French Alpine Club* (C.A.F.) has an office in the

Avenue de la Gare near the station. You can join on the spot. Benefits include a free insurance scheme in case of accident and cheap rates for accommodation in the various mountain huts, called refuges, in the district (and elsewhere in the Alps). The club runs training courses for beginners in conjunction with the Guides' Bureau. Regular excursions for simple mountain climbs take place daily on a weekly programme basis. Some details of these are given in the mountaineering section.

Proficient climbers who wish to improve their technique still further can take part in 'collectives' organised at the headquarters of the famous *French National School for Skiing and Alpinism* (É.N.S.A.). This school is located on the old road to Les Pèlerins, shortly before you reach the Aig. du Midi cableway station.

The *Chamonix Mountain Rescue Society* (S.C.S.M.) has a bureau in the Place du Mt. Blanc, and an extension at the tourist inquiry office. This is a permanent organisation which draws recruits from the register of mountain guides. Rescues are undertaken on a paying basis. Victims of accidents, or their relatives, are held responsible for all expenses. The cost of rescue operations anywhere in the Alps is notoriously expensive and it is a wise precaution to be fully insured before setting off to climb. Even the simplest rescue costs £50 ($120.00). If aircraft are employed, very much more. Club insurances do not as a rule cover the cost of air rescue. This annoying situation is maintained to ensure the maximum employment of mountain guides. You either pay the difference out of your own pocket or are covered by an independent insurance. The aircraft used for mountain rescue work in this district are helicopters.

Summer skiing

The Guides' Bureau organises regular courses of instruction throughout the summer season. These are held on a daily and weekly basis at three locations at the top of high téléphériques: Grands-Montets, Midi/Géant, and the Index. Tariffs include cheap rates on cableways, and all-inclusive instruction with transportation to the skifields.

Chamonix in winter

The valley is a winter sports centre of the 'premier ordre' (three categories are defined by the Government Tourist Office). None the less the skiing is mainly serious and Chamonix is not an ideal place for beginners. The ski-runs are superb. There are several books available in English which give a good outline description of the winter facilities. Being shaded by the Mt. Blanc range to the south, the valley is decidedly cold, and you have to travel frequently on cableways to reach the higher sunny slopes.

There are three ski-jumps, two skating rinks and a first-rate ski school with 40 instructors and 12 marked ski-runs. Ice hockey and curling, bobsleigh and gymkhana competitions are held throughout the season.

Long ski-runs are popular in the spring. The Guides' Bureau organises 'collectives' for the High Level Route from Chamonix to Zermatt, which is probably the most famous overland ski tour in the world; also for the Tour of Mt. Blanc, which circles the Mt. Blanc range. Spring is the best time for the experienced skier who is not particularly interested in competitive sport.

All main roads, rail services and cableways are open in winter.

Holidaymakers in Chamonix

Statue of de Saussure and Balmat, who is pointing the way to summit of Mt. Blanc

Café scene in Ave. de la Gare

Builders' materials stacked on a wall in side street (overleaf)

The town squares have coin-slot telescopes for looking at Mt. Blanc (overleaf, above left)

Ice hockey at the Olympic stadium (overleaf, below left)

Early morning at campsite in Les Pèlerins, with Mt. Blanc appearing through mist (above)

Entrance to Mt. Blanc tunnel, Chamonix end (above right)

Approaching Courmayeur end of Mt. Blanc tunnel (below right)

Alouette II helicopter. Not everyone returns from the mountains under his own steam. Flights in the range cost anything from £20 to £50

Hotels

The official classification scheme for French hotels is complex. It is in four categories on a 'star' rating system. In each category hotels are sub-divided by letters into three further categories, according to a standard for the number of rooms by proportion with private baths available. Broadly speaking the system relates closely to other hotel classification schemes, which may or may not take account of the private baths facility. In France it is possible to have a 'Four Star' hotel with a sub-category 'C'. Travellers with reasonable experience of hotels in Europe will be able to choose without further advice. Category is related fairly closely to price. Consult a tourist office (see Appendices) if you are in doubt and ask for a complete list of hotels in the area.

Range of hotels in Chamonix 1968/9

All-inclusive price per day (in francs) 3 days minimum

		Number	Plain season	July/August
Luxury	A	3	60–120	100–140
	B	1	50–75	70–90
	C	1	50–75	60–90
1st class	A	1	50–70	60–80
	B	1	45–60	55–70
	C	1	45–60	55–70
2nd class	A	9	35–60	40–70
	B	5	30–50	40–60
	C	2	30–50	35–60
3rd class	A	9	30–40	35–45
	B	2	25–40	35–40
	C	4	25–35	25–40

About a dozen hotels are not included in this analysis (classification not agreed). Some hotels in the 3rd class do not have restaurants. There are also many good hotels in the neighbouring villages and hamlets of Le Tour, Argentière, Le Lavancher, Les Praz, Les Bossons, Les Houches and Servoz.

Public services. General amenities

Number	Service	Location
1	**Airfield (local)**	Le Fayet
4	**Banks**	Town centre
1	**Beach**	Lac du Bouchet
1	**Bowling**	Le Chamois (A. de la Gare)
2	**Bus stations**	P. du Mt. Blanc; railway station
7	**Cabarets**	Le Chamois, Le Bivouac, Le Toboggan, Le Pèle, La Niche, La Grange, Le Club Écossais
5	**Carparks**	P. du Mt. Blanc; Le Biollay; R. du Brévent; P. de l'Église; P. Balmat
1	**Casino**	P. Balmat
4	**Chemists**	
2	**Churches**	(Catholic, Protestant)
4	**Cinemas**	Mt. Blanc, Refuge, Casino, Vox
4	**Dentists**	
7	**Doctors**	
1	**Exchange office**	P. de l'Église
many	**Garages**	(car hire)
2	**Golf**	Les Praz; Les Pèlerins
1	**Guides' bureau**	P. de l'Église
1	**Hospital**	R. Joseph Vallot
1	**Ice rink (stadium)**	A. de la Patinoire
2	**Libraries**	Town hall and Payot, P. de la Poste
1	**Municipal shower baths**	La Résidence (A. de la Gare)
several	**Opticians**	
1	**Police station**	R. du Brévent
1	**Post office**	P. de l'Église
30	**Restaurants/ cafés**	
1	**Riding**	Les Praz
1	**Ski-jump**	Aig. du Midi station
1	**Swimming**	Lac du Bouchet
1	**Taxi rank**	railway station
2	**Tennis**	Lac du Bouchet; Majestic hotel
	Town hall	P. de l'Église
	Tourist office	P. de l'Église, ✆ 24
	Travel agent	Catella, A. de la Gare
	Youth hostel (40 beds)	Les Pèlerins

44

Mountain transport, cableways
including Le Fayet/St. Gervais-les-Bains
and descent to Courmayeur

◿ rack-and-pinion (cog) railway	⬒ téléphérique
⌷ télécabine	⬔ télésiège
	Ⴤ téléski

Type	From–to	Altitude lower	upper	Distance from Chamonix (km.)	Francs 1968/9 fares single	return
⬒	**Chamonix–Plan des Aiguilles**	1043	2308		06.25	10.00
⌷	**Plan des Aiguilles–Aiguille du Midi**	2308	3795/ 3842		08.75	15.00
⬒	**Aiguille du Midi–Pte. Helbronner**	3800	3462		15.00	25.00
⬒	**Pte. Helbronner–Torino (Géant)**	3462	3322		Italian	
⬒	**Torino–Pavillon**	3322	2174		Italian	
⬒	**Pavillon–La Palud**	2174	1390		Italian	
	La Palud–Courmayeur (*10 min. by bus*)					
Ⴤ	**Various skilifts in vicinity of Col du Géant**					
◿	**Chamonix–Montenvers**	1040	1913		07.00	12.00
⌷	**Montenvers–Mer de Glace**				02.00	03.00
⬒	**Chamonix–Planpraz**	1040	1999		05.00	08.00
⬒	**Planpraz–Brévent**	1999	2526		03.00	06.00
⬒	**Les Praz–La Flégère**	1060	1890	1·5	05.00	08.00
⌷	**La Flégère–L'Index**	1890	2385		04.00	06.00
Ⴤ	**L'Index skilift**	varies			varies	

Type	From–to	Altitude lower	upper	Distance from Chamonix (km.)	Francs 1968/9 fares single	return
	Les Chosalets–Croix de Lognan	1250	1972	7	04.00	07.00
	Croix de Lognan–Grands Montets	1972	3271		08.00	13.00
	Grands Montets skilifts	varies			varies	
	Argentière–L'Aiguillette	1252	1727	8	03.50	06.00
	Le Tour–Charamillon	1462	1850	12	03.00	06.00
	Charamillon–Col de Balme	1850	2186		03.00	06.00
	Le Tour–Balme					09.00
	Les Bossons–Glacier	1030	1400	3·5	04.00	05.00
	Les Houches–Bellevue	993	1790	8	04.50	08.00
	Col de Vose–Le Prarion	1653	1887		02.30	03.50
	Le Fayet/St. Gervais–Nid d'Aigle (Mt. Blanc Tramway via Col de Vose/ Bellevue)	591	2364	19	12.00	20.00

Can be joined directly from Chamonix by the Bellevue
téléphérique

All mountain transport systems generally operate from
07.00 to 19.00 hours, with a break at lunchtime. The
services are continuous and a longer wait than 15 min. is
unusual.

Mt. Blanc tunnel
from Chamonix to Courmayeur

Regulations
Maximum dimensions of vehicles: height 4·15 m.
(13 ft. 7 in.), length 18 m. (59 ft.), width 2·5 m.
(8 ft. 2 in.), total weight 35 metric tons (34 tons 5 cwt.),

axle weight 13 metric tons (12 tons 15 cwt.). Maximum speed 70 km./h. (43 m.p.h.), minimum speed 50 km./h. (31 m.p.h.). Do not stop or overtake. Keep 100 m. between vehicles. Turn on side and rear lights but not headlights. Breakdown bays with telephones at intervals. Customs and passport control at Italian end.

Charges

Charges	*francs*
Motor cycles :	06.00.
Cars up to 1000 c.c. :	16.00.
1000–1699 c.c. :	24.00.
1700–2399 c.c. :	32.00.
over 2400 c.c. :	40.00.
Trailers or caravans :	08.00
Coaches :	50 to 150.00.

There are reductions for return within three days and special night rates for commercial vehicles.

Mont Blanc

The crowning glory of the Chamonix valley is Mt.
Blanc (4807 m.), the highest mountain in Europe. Of
all the Alpine summits, Mt. Blanc for nearly two
centuries has exercised a greater fascination for
climbers and for tourists in general than any other. If
it has a rival, it could only be the Matterhorn. The first
mention of Mt. Blanc in English is found in Dr.
Thomas Burnet's letters (1685)—the author of a
famous and fanciful work on the theory of the earth's
structure. He speaks of 'the hill called Maudit or
Cursed, two miles in perpendicular height, and of
which one third is always covered with snow'.

The mountain range in which Mt. Blanc rises is
orientated south-west to north-east and is about
35 km. long and 15 km. wide (as between Chamonix
and Courmayeur). The absolute outside limits can be
fixed at the Great and Little St. Bernard passes. The
mountain has a number of important secondary
summits of almost equal height and several
independent peaks in the same range rise over 4000 m.

The frontier between France and Italy follows the
backbone of the range north-east, up to Mt. Dolent
(3823 m.). Beyond this point the range is shared by
France and Switzerland. Altogether the range is
perfectly isolated; in distant views from other parts
of the Alps it is always outstandingly conspicuous,
being compact and higher than any other object on
the horizon.

A fairly broad snow ridge about 150 m. long marks
the summit. As the crow flies the summit is due south
of Chamonix and about 10 km. distant. The Taconnaz
and Bossons glaciers, separated by a spur called the
Montagne de la Côte, stream down the Chamonix
side which is predominantly a complex snowy face.
Huge crevasses and séracs (towers and pinnacles of
ice) break the surface of these glaciers, and similar ice
labyrinths can be seen in all parts of the range.

Temperatures at the summit vary enormously,
although in daytime during the summer the air is
usually above freezing point. Apart from storm
conditions, the most serious hazard for climbers is
wind. The large snowfields under the summit are
notoriously exposed to strong winds which can
penetrate the best clothing in a few seconds and lead
to rapid exhaustion and frostbite. The summit view is
not especially fine because the dome of ice rears high

48

above the range of granite aiguilles and glaciers which might be seen to more advantage from lower points. However, the panorama is very extensive and embraces all the major ranges of the Western Alps. On a clear day Lyon can be seen.

The climb by the usual routes from the Chamonix valley is technically easy, though fairly long and tiring. Considerable stamina is required of persons unaccustomed to serious mountaineering activity. Several huts for climbers are placed in strategical positions on the mountain so that the ascent can be made in comfortable stages. Many hundreds of persons climb the mountain every year, and over 200 have reached the summit on the same day.

The earliest attempts to climb Mt. Blanc were prompted by de Saussure. He explained later: 'During my first attempts from Chamonix in 1760 and 1761 I sent notices to every parish in the valley that I would give a handsome reward to whosoever found a practicable route to the summit.' This announcement led to many attempts in an heroic period lasting 25 years. On 1 July, 1786, Jacques Balmat, having been abandoned by his companions, came within an ace of reaching the top alone. A few weeks later, on 8 August, and accompanied by the village doctor, Michel-Gabriel Paccard, he succeeded after two days' climbing by reaching the *calotte* at six-twenty in the evening!

Balmat's own account, which was not discovered till 1904, says: 'I went for the first time to the Dôme du Goûter on 28 June, 1786, and I went alone. On my way down, towards the foot of the Montagne de la Côte, I met three men also bound on an exploring expedition, who invited me to turn back with them. This I consented to do, went home for provisions, and at 11 o'clock of the evening of the same day once more set out to rejoin them on the summit of the Montagne de la Côte, which I reached at two o'clock next morning. We at once set out and reached the Dôme du Goûter by mid-day. Having been caught in the mist and having seen two men at the top of the Goûter, we called to them and they gave us to understand that they would like to join our party. In the meantime I set out by myself to make the ascent by the Arête Blanche; I got almost to the summit, but could not reach it, owing to mist. Redescending in quest of my comrades, I was unable to find them; they had gone down, leaving me alone. I took heart of grace and once more began the climb, this time by the left side. I managed to get quite close to Mont Blanc, and had a view of the Val d'Aosta. Mont Blanc was completely covered by fog. I was forced to redescend to the Grand Plateau, where night overtook me and where I was brought up by a great crevasse which I had crossed in the morning by way of a feeble bridge of frozen snow. This bridge I could not find in the darkness and fear of being crushed by the ice forced me to retrace my steps to the top of the ridge; there I spent the night, 1455 "toises" above the Priory, my fourth night out of doors. My clothes, and the handkerchief about my face, froze on me. I kept stamping and striking my hands together all night, and having seen that the sun was too feeble to drive away the clouds from the summit of Mont Blanc, I redescended to Chamonix. It was only a few days afterwards that Dr. Paccard invited me to make the same attempt with him, and setting out on 7 August, 1786, we did not reach our goal till six o'clock of the evening. We remained 32 minutes on the summit and then redescended to the Montagne de la Côte, which we reached at 11 o'clock of the evening. On the 9th, we arrived at Chamonix at 8 o'clock of the morning.'

Henceforth the name of Jacques Balmat was on every tongue in the valley and his fame spread far and wide. The title of Mt. Blanc Balmat was conferred on him by the King of Sardinia. The destiny of Chamonix was sealed.

In the following year de Saussure made the second ascent with a party of 18 guides and porters. Six days later he was followed by the Englishman, Col. Mark Beaufoy. The subsequent history of climbing on Mt. Blanc is long and intricate and has been the subject of many erudite works worthy of comparison with the best mystery stories.

Notable events on the mountain include: the erection of a hut and observatory on the Rochers Foudroyés at 4357 m. in 1890 by the scientist and geographer, Jacques Vallot. This hut has been improved several times since and is now a fine but small C.A.F. refuge. A shack was built as an observatory by Dr. Janssen a few metres from the summit in 1893, which in due course sank in the snow. The first ascent of the mountain in winter was made by Miss Arabella Straton with two Chamonix guides on 31 January, 1876. Miss Straton married one of the guides—a well-known and unprecedented event in 19th-century Alpine history. First ascent on ski, by Hugo Mylius and Bernese guides on 25 February, 1904. The mountain was crossed by Spelterini in a balloon in 1909, and later by Parmelin in an aeroplane. In 1921 the Swiss aviator Durafour landed his plane on the Col du Dôme (4250 m.) and managed—only just—to take off again. In 1955 a Bell helicopter alighted on the summit, and this stunt has been repeated in an Alouette III flown from Le Fayet aerodrome.

Finally, in June, 1968, two Chamonix policemen accomplished the astounding feat of climbing the mountain, up and down from the Gendarmerie in the Place de l'Église, in 8 h. 48 min. Needless to say, this time betters the previous record by several hours.

On the way up Mt. Blanc, looking back down the Bossons glacier into the Chamonix valley. Aig. du Midi on right

On the summit of Mt. Blanc (4807 m.). Note the windproof clothing, including over-trousers, thick woollen gloves and small practical sack

Climbers resting at the Goûter hut after an ascent of Mt. Blanc

Section one

Excursions from Chamonix

General considerations

Excursions suitable for a day in the mountains are very numerous. Apart from interesting walks near the town, these fall under two broad headings.
(1) Approaches to glaciers and peaks in the main range. (2) Ascents to viewpoints from where the main range is seen to maximum advantage. For the latter there are several excellent points on the ridge enclosing the north side of the valley, which commands extensive views of the main range on the opposite side. This ridge is called the *Aiguilles Rouges*. Closer viewpoints lie on the rim of the main range .itself directly above the valley.

Excursions are described in order according to their length, starting with short walks from the town and extending gradually to small 'expeditions', for which a full day should be allowed. Routes that start from other centres in the valley are included but are grouped under the headings of two villages : Les Houches and Argentière. Time and transportation to reach these starting points present no problem for visitors staying in Chamonix. Buses or trains go up and down the valley about every 45 min.

The fact of the matter is that the ever-spreading network of cableways has converted many classic walks to an effortless ride high above the footpaths. In result a number of previously less-frequented paths that cross the mountain-sides more or less horizontally are now used as popular high-level connections between cableway stations. For this type of trip the original footpath from the valley to the cableway terminus is described briefly—for those who prefer to walk up all the way, or descend on foot. These paths are generally large, unmistakable and signposted at junctions. Most of them are classed as *chemin muletier* because they were originally constructed to be climbed by laden horses or mules. Narrower footpaths can be confused by sheep tracks or unmarked junctions. In most cases these paths are marked by paint flashes on rocks or wayside trees.

Several recommended excursions are either not served by a cableway for gaining height, or continue much higher than a cableway terminus. Reservations addressed to the ordinary tourist about these outings should be observed in the interests of safety.

Children of the age of 8 to 10 years or more can be

taken on all excursions unless there are indications
to the contrary.

Some cableway stations display a notice daily about
conditions at the top of the line and whether the
mountains and views are obscured by cloud.

Precautions

A consideration in walking up from the valley is to
make an early start. Or at a time when the sun is not
beating down on the slopes. It is always relatively cool
in the lower forested sections, but during the heat of
day flies and insects are a nuisance.

In fine weather a pair of stout walking shoes will be
adequate. In rain some paths are muddy and stony
sections become slippery—when a pair of boots are
more comfortable and drier. Canvas shoes are good
enough for short walks taken from cableway stations.
A walking stick is an asset for any excursion of more
than an hour. A hat or scarf is essential protection
from over-exposure to sun. At an altitude of 2500 m.
or higher the air temperature drops quickly after
16.00 hours. Indeed, in the early morning or late
afternoon at this height is is advisable to have a warm
sweater for sitting in the open air. After sunset it is
decidedly chilly at this altitude. Sun glasses are
optional, according to the needs of the individual, but
should be worn at all times on glaciers and snow.

A further point about the highest cableways.
Visitors with delicate tummies can suffer from mild
forms of mountain sickness when transported swiftly
to heights over 3000 m. This is mainly due to lack of
acclimatisation, i.e. the absence of a gradual approach
to condition the respiratory organs to rarefied air.
(Walking up from the bottom is a reliable way of
avoiding mountain sickness.) The symptoms are quick
breathing, slight dizziness, headache or sickness. None
are the least dangerous. The remedy is to descend,
when the sickness soon disappears. While only very
few people are affected, it is not wise to eat large
amounts of food (especially sweet delicacies), say at the
upper station of the Aig. du Midi. The restaurant may
tempt you to over-indulge, with unpleasant
consequences. Of course, after a few days you can
be so well acclimatised that anything goes on the
menu !

For those routes—the most ambitious excursions
in this part of the guidebook—that cross dry glaciers,

i.e. those with no covering of snow, you should have a walking stick with a spike fitted to the bottom. This comes in handy for walking up inclines of ice. Though rough and affording a good grip underfoot, the surface of such slopes can suddenly and for no obvious reason manifest slippery patches. These glacier routes are perfectly safe if ordinary precautions are observed. Keep away from the edge of crevasses if the edge is not sharply defined. Do not step on patches of old snow lying near crevasses on a glacier. Sunbathing on glaciers is extremely dangerous and only arms and legs should be exposed.

On glaciers there is no path to indicate the way. You should line up the direction in which you walk with an object near the correct place you wish to reach on the far side. Exercise care while crossing stones (moraine) at the edge of a glacier. These have a nasty habit of rolling away underfoot after a few hours of hot sun has loosened them from the icy surface beneath.

Maps

Several maps for excursionists can be bought in Chamonix. A map is recommended for appreciating the layout of the district and is an endless source of informative instruction, for planning excursions or for passing away the time.

The best general map for tourists which is usually available in large cities of countries like Britain and the United States is the tourist production entitled *Massif du Mont-Blanc*, published by Didier & Richard of Grenoble in France. This map is drawn to a scale of 1 : 50,000 (about $1\frac{1}{4}$ in. to one mile), is based on the French Government Survey and has specially overprinted lines which indicate walking routes in various categories, ski itineraries, and dangerous places. Government maps of 1 : 50,000 and 1 : 20,000 can also be bought. In Britain all the maps can be obtained from West Col Productions, 1 Meadow Close, Goring on Thames, Reading, Berks.

A bookshop specialising in topographical publications of Chamonix is: Librairie Les Étoiles, 46 Avenue de la Gare.

CMB—D

1 Short walks from town

Bouchet lake

In the previous review of the main facilities of
Chamonix, passing mention has been made of the
beach at the Bouchet lake and woods. From the Ave.
de la Gare go along the Ave. du Bouchet, cross the
Pl. du Mt. Blanc and take either of the forked roads
on the other side. The Bouchet road continues right,
the Ave. de la Patinoire left, past the ice rink and
stadium. Both lead to the lake in 15 min. The wood
is combed with small paths, inevitably crowded on a
fine day.

Paradis des Praz

A road round the south-east side of the Bouchet
wood eventually crosses the Arveyron stream, beside
the railway bridge, and turns north-west to join the
main road bridge in the valley at Les Praz.
Alternatively, from the lake a footpath follows the
left bank of the Arve to the bridge at Les Praz. Here,
on your right, is another lake ; the golf course and La
Flégère cableway station are straight ahead across the
main road. A small road leads off right (north) from
the cableway station. It crosses the River Arve and
you come to a restaurant at the lower edge of an
idyllic wood called the Paradis des Praz. This is a very
popular picnic venue favoured with a stunning view
of the Drus and Chamonix Aiguilles. 2 h.

   From Chamonix the most direct way to the Paradis
des Praz is to follow the main road (Rue J. Vallot). By
bus or train to Les Praz, then on foot, 20 min.

Source of the Arveyron

The Arveyron is the wide stream draining from the
end of the Mer de Glace, the actual tip of which is
known as the Glacier des Bois, so called because in
the 19th century it extended almost into the trees
below. The stream is only a few kilometres long before
it joins the River Arve behind the Bouchet wood.
Most of its course in the bottom has been engineered
with reinforced banks to prevent flooding. For so
short a stream it carries a great deal of water, being
the outfall for the largest catchment basin in the
Mt. Blanc range. Many years ago a huge ice cavern
could be inspected in the snout of the glacier, from
where the water poured forth into the open.
Subsequent changes in the glacier, due to recession,

have removed the novelty of this spectacle. The moraine below the glacier is overgrown with shrubs and pine trees and there are paths across it.

Follow the road to the Bouchet wood and continue beside the railway to where both cross the Arveyron. Without crossing the bridge, a footpath passes under the railway and follows the stream bank along the edge of the Ortha woods (large rock). At the next bridge cross the stream and reach the outskirts of the village called Les Bois. Turn right and continue along a good path on the other side of the stream; keep right at junctions. In a short distance reach a small café where the stream tumbles over rocks from the glacier above. Good view of the Drus. 2 h., or 40 min. from Praz station.

Ruskin's Stone
An isolated rock with a bronze plaque inscribed to the memory of the artist and philosopher, John Ruskin (1819–1900), who often visited the Chamonix valley. As an 'apostle of the religion of mountain beauty' he is claimed to have chosen this spot to make notes for his work, *Of Mountain Beauty*. He was the first artist to draw Alpine peaks in their true perspective and he wrote vividly about the mystical impressions conveyed by mountains.

From the tourist office in the Pl. de l'Église follow the road to the Brévent cableway station. Take a footpath on the left and follow this pleasantly to the stone. Seats in the sun facing south and a splendid view of the valley with Mt. Blanc towering overhead. 20 min.

Les Gaillands lake
An artificial construction in the woods between the main road and railway beside Les Pèlerins station. The main road or an obvious secondary parallel road through the suburbs of Les Rebats and Les Pècles can be used to reach the lake, about 45 min. from the centre. Against the slope to the west of the main road are practice rocks for climbers, and behind these footpaths twist through the forest up to the Plan Lacha chalets (1574 m.).

Cascade du Dard
The huge tarmac platform at the entrance to the Mt. Blanc tunnel now adjoins this picturesque spot. The

waterfall lies directly above the last but one zigzag on the access road to the tunnel.

From Chamonix take the back road to Les Pèlerins, past the Aig. du Midi cableway station to Les Barats. Now fork left along a slip road to Les Tissours. The bypass road is crossed by an underground passageway. On the other side a well-marked path (fork right) climbs into the forest and leads close to the first and second bends in the tunnel access road to a café at a corner where the waterfall is seen in a ravine; two pitches of 13 m. and 50 m. About 1 h.

You can drive or go by bus to the tunnel entrance. There is parking immediately below on left. A path leaves the carpark and traverses the forest below the ancient Midi cableway, close to a double pylon. 10 min. You can also reach the café down a staircase starting from the platform itself (extreme left-hand side).

A pleasant way back on foot is to descend the original footpath from carpark below platform to Les Pèlerins; the path crosses zigzags in the access road three times before you reach the first houses of the village. Among these on the left is the chalet in which Jacques Balmat was born (1762); it is open to the public; souvenirs of the first ascent of Mt. Blanc.

A finer return route is to take the footpath opposite the carpark, climb the embankment and follow this across the Creuse bridge to the Cerro café (1358 m.) overlooking the snout of the Bossons glacier. 15 min. From here descend directly towards Les Bossons; on reaching a road junction you can turn right along a footpath which crosses the Creuse stream to Les Pèlerins. For round trip from Chamonix, allow $2\frac{1}{2}$ h.

Note: a delightful excursion on the Bossons glacier is described in the section dealing with the chairlift of the same name.

2 Principal mountain railway & cableway excursions

Unlike ordinary railways, cableways are restricted in the placing of lower stations by design and engineering requirements. They must usually start from a point directly below the height to which the system rises. This may mean that you must go on foot, or by car or train, to the site of the lower station.

There are three mountain transport systems more or less on the outskirts of Chamonix: the Montenvers railway, and the Brévent and Aig. du Midi cableways.

The first two undoubtedly serve the most popular scenic observation points above the resort. The third is even finer, though quite expensive.

In 1741 Windham and Pococke were the first complete strangers to visit the Montenvers. De Saussure made the first tourist ascent of the Brévent in 1760, during the first of his many visits to the valley. The Brévent is still climbed quite frequently on foot and is an easy but fairly long walk. Before the cableway the Aig. du Midi could only be attained by climbers. The long-awaited completion in 1955 of the téléphérique system to the lower of the two rock knobs forming the summit was hailed as the most notable engineering feat of its kind in the Alps.

Montenvers (sta. 1913 m., hotel 1909 m.)
In Chamonix the rack railway adjoins the main station and is reached by a footbridge. Trains operate up and down every 15 or 20 min., between 07.30 and 20.00 h. The journey is mainly through forest with a notable section in a curved tunnel. For appreciating fine views into the valley as the train rises steeply, take a seat on the left-hand side of the carriage, facing up the line. The electric rail coach can haul two others at the same time; the gradient is fairly constant, about 1 in $2\frac{1}{2}$, and the journey takes 20 min. each way.

For walking up to the Montenvers, leave the station and use the footbridge to the Montenvers station. Take its access road leading to the main bypass road which is crossed to a large open area used as a carpark. Cross this to the far side, but do not turn right beside a café-restaurant, leading up a lane to the Biollay. Continue straight ahead along an unmade road to Les Mouilles. Further down on the right is a signposted path; follow this through the forest, with a café half-way up, crossing the rack railway three times. As you emerge from the forest the Dru is an impressive object ahead, but the famous Montenvers panorama is not seen till you reach the hotel. It is warm work uphill in the forest after 11 a.m., so it is preferable to start early. Easy and pleasant in descent. 2–$2\frac{1}{2}$ h. from Chamonix.

The Montenvers hotel is situated conspicuously on a large open terrace above the Mer de Glace. The zoological enclosure is behind the hotel (entrance fee). Directly opposite soars the granite obelisk of the Petit Dru, standing in front of the higher Aig. Verte. This is

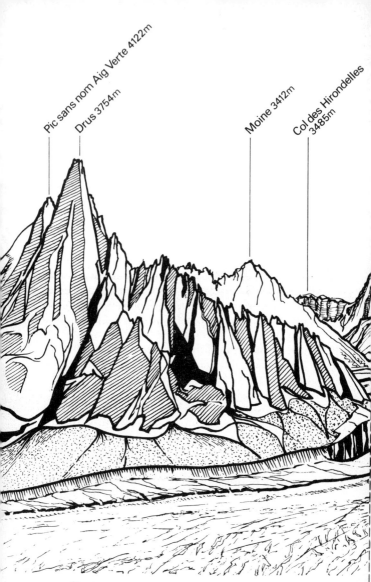

Pic sans nom Aig Verte 4122m

Drus 3754m

Moine 3412m

Col des Hirondelles 3485m

East

Mer de Glace panorama from the Montenvers

64

Grandes Jorasses 4208m

Dôme de Rochefort 4015m

Mt Mallet 3989m

Aig du Géant 4013m

République 3305m

Grands Charmoz 3444m

Blaitière 3522

South

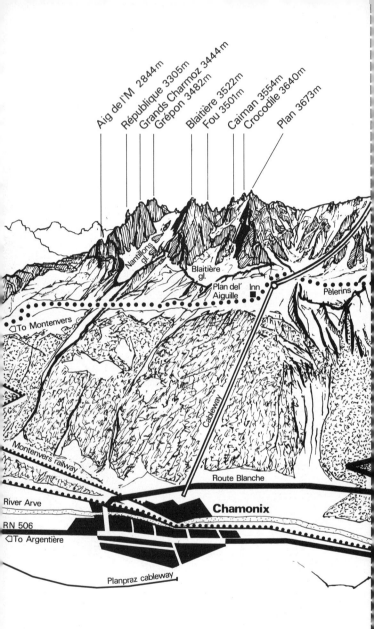

Aig de l'M 2844m
République 3305m
Grands Charmoz 3444m
Grépon 3482m
Blaitière 3522m
Fou 3501m
Caiman 3554m
Crocodile 3640m
Plan 3673m

Nantillons gl.

Blaitière gl.

Plan del' Aiguille

Inn

Pèlerins

To Montenvers

Cableway

Montenvers railway

Route Blanche

River Arve

Chamonix

RN 506

To Argentière

Planpraz cableway

Chamonix Aiguilles & Mont Blanc from the Brevent

66

Aig du Midi 3842m

Mt Blanc du Tacul 4248m

Mt Maudit 4465m

Mt Blanc 4807m

Dôme du Goûter 3863m

Aig du Goûter 3863m

St - Gervais Route

glacier

Grands Mulets

Plan Glacier

modern approach

Bossons glacier

Montagne de la Côte

Taconnaz glacier

Cascade du Dard

Tunnel

Chairlift

Balmat-Paccard approach

Route Blanche

Les Pèlerins

Les Bossons

RN 506

River Arve

RN 506

possibly the most competitive peak for rock climbers in the Mt. Blanc range. From the restaurant terrace a powerful telescope can be used to watch the progress of parties on the mountain. Looking straight up the glacier you see the north face of the Grandes Jorasses, a wall of rocks and ice with an equally famous climbing history. Framing the panorama further right, the Aig. des Grands Charmoz rises in splendid isolation. It forms one end of the Chamonix Aiguilles. A sketch of the panorama appears on pages 64, 65.

The hotel has two classes of accommodation, rather dear, and large indoor and outdoor restaurants. Bunkhouse accommodation in a nearby annexe. Well worth staying overnight.

The mountain path from Chamonix is one of the oldest in the district. It was used by crystal hunters who made sorties up the Mer de Glace and foraged along the flanking mountains for rock crystals which they brought down in abundance from the glacial junctions at the Talèfre and Leschaux ice streams. Though not precious stones in the proper sense, in the 18th and 19th centuries these attractive rock crystals fetched high prices. A lot of them were used to decorate cabinets and vanity boxes. Samples can be seen at the hotel (and imitations are sold at nearby souvenir booths!).

A shepherds' hut was found at the Montenvers by Windham's party. Then an Englishman called Blair provided money in 1779 for another 'miserable hovel'. It had the words 'Utile dulci' carved over the door and was dubbed grandiosely the Château du Montenvers (or de Blair). It was composed of boulder stone and dry wall turfed over. A more substantial hut was erected in 1795 at the instigation of Bourrit, 'to receive the learned men who came there and to contain the instruments necessary for the observation of these rare beauties of nature'. Thus it was christened the *Temple of Nature*, but it seems to have been mainly used by muleteers as a drinking room. The first inn was built in 1840 and this was enlarged to an hotel in 1879. The railway arrived in 1908.

The large slab-rock called the *Pierre des Anglais*, where Windham's party is alleged to have taken shelter, will be found somewhat below the hotel.

The Montenvers ('the mountain facing north') is

really only a grassy shoulder above the left bank of the lower part of the **Mer de Glace.** At this point it is some 650 m. wide. Many important approaches to mountain huts in the heart of the range start here. Recently a télécabine system has been installed to take visitors down to the glacier in 330 m. However, it can be reached easily on foot by a wide path leading from the railway terminus in a few zigzags. The lower section has fixed handrails. 15 min. The glacier is bare ice with a rough granulated surface. On the part where tourists gather it is not slippery. There are large open crevasses both a little higher and lower than the point where the path finishes. A cave has been dug in the ice, through which you can pass for a small payment into the bowels of the glacier. Here you can examine in artificial light the underground foldings of ice caused by movement and pressure. The glacier 'flows' at approximately 1 cm. per hour, or 90 m. a year. Standing on its surface you are not of course aware of this fact !

Much of our knowledge of the laws and causes of glacier motion is due to observations made on the Mer de Glace during the 19th century by Principal Forbes and Professor John Tyndall, who spent many weeks in the squalid 'Temple of Nature' (see above), which was their headquarters.

Helicopters can land on the glacier below the Montenvers.

Le Brévent (2526 m.)
This is a rocky promontory in the range of small peaks called the Aiguilles Rouges, enclosing the north-west side of the valley. It commands an unrivalled view of the north side of Mt. Blanc and indeed of the entire range. On foot it is quite a long walk, although either the first or second stages of the cableway can be used to break the climb or descent.

The cableway is situated 5 min. from the Pl. de l'Église, on the opposite side of the town from the railway station.

This is Chamonix's original 'grande remontée mécanique'. It was built in 1928 and the first stage rises over six pylons above forest and clearings for 900 m. to *Plan Praz*, which is reached in 9 min. You change to a smaller télécabine and the second section zooms in another direction, finally climbing in front of the sheer precipice of the Brévent where the sense of height and space is tremendous. The cables are drawn in one unsupported length of 1350 m., rising 500 m. between Plan Praz and the top. Restaurant, shop and hotel.

On foot there are two distinct paths.

Rather shorter but steeper is the Plan Praz route. Start beside the cableway station, pass Ruskin's Stone and go up directly in the forest to the Plan des Chablettes restaurant (1545 m.), then in many zigzags over pasture to Plan Praz. The hotel is above the cableway station at 2062 m. From this point the panorama of the Mt. Blanc range is almost as fine as from the top. 3 h. from Chamonix.

Leave Plan Praz by keeping left of the hotel along a well-marked path winding south-west and north-west round a spur; ignore a right fork to the Col du Brévent. The path eventually bears south-west across a stony hollow and climbs to a rockface. Go up this in an easy chimney of 17 m. with fixed handrail and on to the ridge above. The chimney can be avoided by a circuitous route to the right. The summit of the Brévent is a few min. higher, and the cairn is situated about 20 m. above the cableway terminus. About $1\frac{1}{2}$ hr. from Plan Praz, or $4\frac{1}{2}$ h. from Chamonix.

The more roundabout route, though less fatiguing and taking an hour longer, starts along the road leading south-west from the cableway station. Take the first right fork up to a good path coming along from Ruskin's Stone. This path slants across the forested mountain-side (keep right at a major junction) to the Plan Lacha. From here continue by easy slopes to the *Bellachat inn* (2151 m.) on the ridge of the Aigs. Rouges, up which the path on the far side of the crest is followed to the top. The summit of the Brévent has easy slopes on all sides except for a vertical rockface overlooking Chamonix.

It is essential to visit the Brévent on a clear day to reap the glorious vista of the Mt. Blanc range. The premier mountain itself is most prominent of all—a series of icy domes skirted by huge snowfields, and with glaciers trailing down towards the valley. End to end, the jagged crests of the Chamonix Aiguilles fill the sky directly opposite, with the cableway rising from the valley floor to the highest point at the Aig. du Midi. Many popular climbs can be traced in every particular on Mt. Blanc and the Aiguilles. The telescopes provided are invariably trained on the

St. Gervais Route, which is seen in profile to the right of the summit of Mt. Blanc. Further left the Mer de Glace curls round the corner below the Montenvers, dominated by the Drus and Aig. Verte. Leftwards again the Grands Montets cableway climbs broad slopes of the Lognan to the foot of the Aig. Verte. Then jutting up like sharks' fins on the next ridge are the Aigs. du Chardonnet and d'Argentière; further back are the popular training peaks of the Aigs. du Tour. At the head of the valley the Col de Balme with its chairlift system is plainly seen.

The scenery in the opposite direction, extending north to west, has a special limestone character. The tilted snow-table summit of the Buet is most conspicuous; from it there seems to radiate range upon range of shattered limestone ridges, fading into the distance. In the valley below on this side are the upper reaches of the Diose gorge. At each end of the Chamonix valley you can see the Bernese Oberland in one direction and the Dauphiné Alps in the other.

An outline sketch of the panorama for the main range appears on pages 66, 67.

Those who may decide to walk up and down are recommended to ascend by the Bellachat Route and descend via Plan Praz. This is an exceptionally rewarding excursion for good hill-walkers and will occupy a whole day.

Plan des Aiguilles Rouges. The Brévent and its intermediate station at Plan Praz have a rival for unfolding the fabulous spectacle of the Mt. Blanc range; La Flégère. This is a terraced pasture at about the same height as Plan Praz and further north. It is reached by its own cableway (see later). An up-and-down footpath runs from *Plan Praz to La Flégère* and is often used for an afternoon stroll between the two stations. It is the first section of a long, scenic high-level traverse across the Chamonix valley slope of the Aigs. Rouges, called the Plan des Aiguilles Rouges. It can be left conveniently at various points to rejoin the valley, or continued to the Col des Montets on the main road at the head of the valley. It is now part of the modern way of doing the famous Tour du Mt. Blanc, a circular walk right round the Mt. Blanc range.

The section between Plan Praz and La Flégère is full of variety and interest. From Plan Praz the path follows open slopes to the north and north-east, working across the head of a large gully and descending slightly round a shoulder to the Charlano chalets (1812 m.). A little further the path forks; keep right, crossing slopes horizontally till at the upper edge of the forest you join the zigzag path coming up from Les Praz–Chamonix to La Flégère. Continue climbing the last zigzags of this path and by keeping left at junctions reach the inn and station at La Flégère. About $1\frac{3}{4}$ h. from Plan Praz.

All along this traverse path there are superb views of the main range, but especially of the Chamonix Aiguilles and Mer de Glace.

Aiguille du Midi (3802 m.)
This téléphérique system is the highest in the world, though contrary to claims it is not the longest continuous passenger cableway. Its construction faced a great deal of opposition, especially the continuation across the Vallée Blanche to the Col du Géant at the Italian frontier. It is doubtful whether the system has spoiled the enjoyment for mountaineers, who were the main objectors. Possibly climbing on the Aig. du Midi itself, which has a number of excellent routes, can be embarrassing. The alpinist can be greeted on top by a horde of tourists full of naïve curiosity, or he may feel uncomfortable while climbing on the north side of the mountain with the cableway swinging overhead.

Originally plans were made to string a cable system from the valley to the Col du Plan, somewhat below the peak. An intermediate station called the Gare des Glaciers, between the Pèlerins and Bossons glaciers, was opened in 1927. A pilot line was finally raised to the col in 1938, where an observatory was built for scientific studies. Then it was discovered that the rock base at the top was too unstable to support the tension of a full cable. War came and the project was abandoned. In any case the bottom station of this proposed line was probably too distant from Chamonix. The new cableway starts from the outskirts. All the pylons of the old system are still standing and the station of the Gare des Glaciers is something of an unsightly relic.

The upper station of the new cableway is excavated in the lower of the two summits of the Aig. du Midi. Tunnels and a covered bridge which spans a dizzy drop into the gap lead to a terrace about 40 m. below the highest peak. In a vertical shaft a lift which can carry 30 persons takes you in 30 seconds to the summit (3842 m.). This was formerly a Grade III rock climb! A television transmission aerial puts another 15 m. on the altitude. The Midi–Géant departure station is found on the terrace overlooking the Vallée Blanche. This balcony also gives access to a swing gate and a short snow ridge leading on to the glacier of the Vallée Blanche for summer skiing. The ordinary tourist should remain on these observation platforms annexed to the upper station complex. Unless you are properly equipped and familiar with glacier terrain you are not advised to venture along the ridge leading down to the glacier. Warnings about the dangers are posted at the station.

At the midway station on the Plan de l'Aiguille there are picturesque walks to be taken below the impressive rock and ice walls of the Aiguilles. These are among the best excursions in the district and require little effort. The longer ones are described in the next section of the guidebook.

To reach the station in the valley, go along the back road leading to Les Pèlerins; 10 min. on foot from the Pl. de Saussure. Large carpark. Cablecars on the first section travel at 40 km./h. through a vertical interval of 1280 m. and can carry 70 persons. The journey takes 8 min. The *Plan de l'Aiguille station* (2317 m.) is placed a short way above the well-known inn of the same name (10 min. on foot lower down). The inn is perched at 2200 m. on a corner in a fine position overlooking the town. The scenery is splendid and the spectator is close enough to the frontal peaks of the range to appreciate the fantastic rock forms displayed by the Chamonix Aiguilles. The ordinary routes on the north side of Mt. Blanc are seen to advantage and there are telescopes at the station restaurant. Also visible, in opposite directions, are the Dauphiné Alps and Bernese Oberland. A short way to the east is the charming Lac Verte (2299 m.), a favourite picnic spot.

To reach the Plan de l'Aiguille on foot from Chamonix involves a long uphill walk through the forest, in countless zigzags. The well-marked mule path starts above the Pèlerins road, at Les Tissours. Having gone through the passageway under the bypass road, take the left fork on the other side (right for Cascade du Dard). About 3½ h.

Plan de l'Aiguille. Most recommendable to those

who do not continue to the Aig. du Midi is to follow the broad traverse path from the Plan de L'Aiguille inn to the Montenvers. This contours a huge terrace some distance below the fretwork skyline of the Aiguilles. The walk is easier in this direction because the path more or less descends gradually all the way. From the cableway station first go down a small path to the right (east) of the pylons; in a few minutes it drops steeply to the inn (a friendly place, good food, modest rates, worth while staying overnight). Here you join the traverse path which cuts across the mountain-side to the north-east. The route is unmistakable. Keep left at any prominent junctions where a branch path may fork uphill. The last section, about 20 min. before arriving at the Montenvers, is one of the prettiest stretches of footpath in the Alps. About $1\frac{3}{4}$ h. from Plan de l'Aiguille inn to Montenvers station.

A traverse below the Chamonix Aiguilles at a much higher level—used by climbers to approach some of the best peaks in the group—is recommended to good walkers. This is described in the next section.

Midi cableway—upper section

Travelling in the small télécabines on the top section of the cableway is a remarkable experience. You are lifted nearly 1500 m. over a distance of 2·87 km. in 6 min. There is no intermediate support for the cables between the Plan de l'Aiguille and Aig. du Midi. With incredible steadiness you rise in front of the immense ice-grooved rock wall of the mountain, and the void beneath the car will set pulses racing. At the top you are met by a vast dazzling amphitheatre of snow nestling under the highest pinnacled crests of Mt. Blanc. The view extends across all the glaciers feeding the Mer de Glace, and on the frontier ridge behind them the Aig. du Géant and Grandes Jorasses are prominent objects. This is about as close as you can get to sharing the reality of the mountain world with the climber, without expending an ounce of energy.

Vallée Blanche–Géant–Courmayeur cableways

Visitors staying in Chamonix are often content with a ride on the cableway to the Aig. du Midi. It is possible to continue much further, and indeed cross the Mt. Blanc range to Courmayeur. This is, as it were, an aerial overhead alternative to the tunnel. The first stage of this extraordinary line crosses the glaciers to the Col du Géant—the most important glacier pass over the Mt. Blanc range from Chamonix to Courmayeur. On a fine day the scenery in all directions is magnificent, and as the journey takes 30 min. you have ample time to enjoy it. A few years ago this section of the line was the scene of a terrible accident. A French Air Force jet fighter flew a few metres over the cable and sonic vibration bounced a number of cars off the fixed wire. The towing cable broke and the result was that cars fell to the glacier 200 m. below, killing the occupants. Other cars further along the cable were stranded in mid-air and passengers spent a cold night at 3500 m. before they could be towed to safety. Needless to say the Air Force has been banned from flying in the Géant glacier basin. ('Shooting up' the cableway had apparently been a frequent practice trick before the accident.)

The line was opened in 1958 and is 5·2 km. long from the Aig. du Midi to Pointe Helbronner, adjacent to the Col du Géant. It crosses the Vallée Blanche to a huge rock called the Gros Rognon (3541 m.), jutting up at the edge of the next section which carries you high over the Géant glacier to Helbronner (3462 m.). Each tiny cabin has a complement of four persons and 36 cabins can operate simultaneously along the line.

At Helbronner station there are summer skiing facilities. After customs examination you can continue along a short cableway to the Torino/Géant hut and station, shop, etc. (3322 m.), from where a 5-min. walk in snow leads to a large hotel on the Col du Géant. It is also possible to walk down snow and rocks from Helbronner to the hotel in a few minutes, but tourists without proper equipment should avoid this unless the prepared path is in good condition.

From the Torino station a full-scale téléphérique descends in two stages via the Mt. Fréty Pavillon to La Palud in the Italian Val Ferret, not far from Courmayeur.

3 Other cableway excursions from Chamonix

In the immediate vicinity of the town there is a major téléphérique system from Les Praz on the Argentière road to La Flégère and the Index, and in the other direction a chairlift to the Bossons glacier. Cableway systems starting from Les Houches and Argentière, in the lower and upper parts of the valley respectively, are described later in the guidebook.

La Flégère–Index (2385 m.)

As indicated previously in the description of the Brévent, this line mounts the Aigs. Rouges slope of the valley, opposite the main range. At the top station of the Index summer skiing is possible from a comparatively low altitude by virtue of shaded north-facing slopes, up which portable skitows can be placed.

Reach the bottom station at Les Praz in the Argentière direction by train or bus in 10 min. The first stage is a large conventional téléphérique, opened in 1955. It ends near the hotel on the open terrace of La Flégère (1890 m.); journey time, 5 min. This very popular vantage point has recently assumed the name of Super-Chamonix.

The easiest route on foot is the tourist path constructed in 1902; this is much more gradual than the older mule path starting closer to Les Praz. From Chamonix start along the main Argentière road to a short way past the hospital. Turn left up an unmade road, then cross the outer boundary road and continue bearing right (north) into the forest. Pass a generating station and follow the obvious path across the forested mountain-side to the Floria (1337 m.) and Violes (1534 m.) cafés. From the last join the zigzag mule path climbing the forest to La Flégère; keep right at junctions. About 3 h.

The panorama of the Mt. Blanc range is more complete than the view obtained from Planpraz (Brévent). La Flégère is directly opposite the Mer de Glace, and the spires of the Drus and Aig. Verte have a particularly bold aspect. Mt. Blanc is equally fine and remains the dominating feature of the scene.

From La Flégère you can return to Chamonix by the traverse path leading to Planpraz, described on page 71; an easy walk, somewhat uphill in this direction, with superb views of Mt. Blanc. In the opposite direction (north-east) the Plan des Aigs. Rouges traverse path continues towards Argentière and the Col des Montets, at two levels according to where you wish to descend towards the valley. Both are easy and in the upper part of the valley you return to Chamonix by bus or train: 2 to 3 h. from La Flégère.

Probably the most popular walk from La Flégère is to *Lac Blanc* and its chalet-hotel. This picturesque lake is locked in a rocky hanging valley under the highest summit of the Aigs. Rouges—the Belvédère. There are two ways of reaching the hotel; either by a good mule path from La Flégère, or by a traverse path from the head of the second stage of the Index cableway. The latter is shorter. This excursion is highly recommended. A cheap cableways and combined meal vouchers ticket is sold by the tourist office for a round trip as follows: Brévent cableway to Planpraz; walk from Planpraz to La Flégère; cableway to the Index terminus; from there walk to Lac Blanc, then descend on foot direct to La Flégère again; cableway down to Les Praz and Chamonix.

The Index cableway is a télécabine system. It was opened in 1956. From La Flégère it rises in 8 min. to 2385 m. at the edge of a stony hanging valley which higher up holds a considerable amount of snow in summer (Index snowfields). Continuation skitows, etc. The Index itself is a rock peak to the west. At the terminal station the view across the valley into the Mer de Glace basin is especially fine.

Lac Blanc. From the upper station of the Index follow a much improved stony path to the north-north-east. It crosses the entrance to the large hanging valley in which the Index snowfields lie. After crossing a stream you pass below cliffs, round the end of a broad ridge and soon join the path coming up from La Flégère, only a few minutes from Lac Blanc. 1 h.

From La Flégère start along the traverse path which contours north to a water source channel. Cross this and a few minutes later take a left fork beside a chalet. Zigzag up grassy slopes to an upper group of chalets, beside the water channel. The path follows the latter all the way to the lake and hotel. 2 h. from La Flégère.

In its rocky trough the lake is sometimes frozen; otherwise on a fine day it provides a beautiful reflection of the Mt. Blanc range. People stay at the chalet-hotel to see the sunrise over the mountains.

Anyone who feels like continuing from Lac Blanc to the lower line of the Plan des Aigs. Rouges and the Col des Montets can do so by taking the small but excellent path which descends gradually due west to the main traverse path, which is joined directly above Argentière in the valley below.

Bossons chairlift and glacier

This is one of the newest mechanical mountaineers at Chamonix. It only reaches 1400 m., but this is far enough for it is designed not so much to afford a breathtaking view as to make the Bossons glacier more accessible for the ordinary tourist.

The chairlift is about 12 min. walk from Les Bossons railway station. The access road passes under the bypass road to the south-west of the village. A bus can be taken all the way. The upper terminus of the chairlift is at a corner in the large path up the Montagne de la Côte, above the chalet-restaurant of the *Grotte* (1298 m.), which is the usual halting place for admiring the glacier. You can descend to it in a few minutes.

The walk up to the chalet is easy and agreeable. From the station turn right down the main road in the village, then take the first road on the left (you continue further down to the chairlift access road). This leads across the bypass road to a Y fork. Keep right and in a few minutes reach a signposted path forking left. Climb this steeply in zigzags through a splendid pine forest immediately above the glacier to the chalet-restaurant. About 1 h.

The torn surface of this cataract-like ice stream has been known to display ice pinnacles 50 m. high. At the head of the glacier you see Mt. Blanc du Tacul and the Aig. du Midi. From the restaurant terrace a path leads down to the left bank of the glacier where a cave has been excavated in the ice (admission fee), about 80 m. deep inside. This is also a favourable point at which to cross the glacier to the right bank. The crossing is perfectly easy and safe but it is only suitable for unguided persons with experience of glacier terrain. Awkward bits (if any) are generally prepared with steps cut in the ice. 30–45 min. On the far side you reach the Cerro café (1358 m.) and can continue to the Cascade du Dard (page 61) or descend to Les Bossons or Les Pèlerins (Jacques Balmat's birthplace).

Another interesting stroll is to follow the path up the Montagne de la Côte to the *Pyramides chalet* (refreshments, etc.), named after the pinnacled glacier, at 1895 m. At two points the path touches the crest between the Bossons and Taconnaz glaciers; unusual view of the latter with its curious enclosing walls of sheer rubble. The Pyramides chalet stands at a corner overlooking the Bossons glacier. $1\frac{1}{2}$ h. from top of chairlift. The sÃ©racs of the glacier gleam with translucent greens and blues. At this level a natural terrace enables the glacier to be crossed without difficulty (45 min., see warning above). On the other side a path in the forest is followed down to the Cerro cafÃ©.

The path continuing to the top of the Montagne de la CÃ´te and the site of Balmat's bivouac is steep and tiring except for good walkers. It was made by the C.A.F. because of the historic importance in early attempts on Mt. Blanc. This approach to the mountain is never used nowadays. The path is taken in descent by a recommended glacier tour described later in the guidebook.

4 Classic mountain walks

These walks usually occupy a whole day; they are scenically superb and always exhilarating. In the main they lie on the principal range and have long traversing sections where the rise and fall of ground is slight. On the other side of the valley, longer walks than those already described on the Aigs. Rouges are mentioned briefly. Apart from not starting out with inadequate clothing or footwear, or in doubtful weather, the most important point to remember is to walk slowly and steadily. Refrain from stopping frequently. The secret of tireless Alpine walking is a steady measured pace, and the duration of these excursions is calculated accordingly. Ample allowances are made for halts in places where it is convenient and pleasant to have a rest. In some cases it is advantageous to sleep at the starting point, by going up the day before.

From Montenvers

Montenvers–Mer de Glace–Chapeau

Historically this is one of the two most famous glacier excursions in the district, the other being the long walk up the centre of the Mer de Glace to the Jardin. As a piece of exercise the Chapeau excursion is both shorter and easier. Crossing the Mer de Glace offers no difficulty, but stout shoes, properly shod, or boots should be worn. Spiked walking stick useful. The once feared Mauvais Pas is absolutely safe, but care should be taken in rain. Montenvers to Chamonix, $3\frac{1}{2}$ h.

Descend the path alongside the railway station and souvenir stalls to the edge of the glacier. Starting a little below the ice cave, cross the glacier on a slightly descending line, bearing exactly north-east. The distance across the ice is 800 m. The path you join on the far side cannot be seen until the last moment. A feature to aim for on the mountain-side above the opposite bank is a vague zigzag track which climbs through wet rock barriers. The point at which you should reach the other side is about 200 m. further right (south). On arriving here there is often a network of open crevasses to weave through before stepping on to large blocks. Cross these diagonally left and reach the crest of the moraine above the glacier (1830 m.). Cairns and path. Grand view of the Chamonix Aiguilles on other side of glacier. 45 min.

Follow the path on the moraine below the wet rock barriers, then rise a little to cross the Nant Blanc stream (waterfall above) by a ledge under a bulging rock (1782 m.). Continue down the moraine immediately above the glacier to the smooth rockface of the *Mauvais Pas*, which no longer deserves its name. The ledge across it has steps hewn in the rock and fixed handrails. Many years ago cows were driven up this path to a summer pasture at the base of the Drus. As it was not practicable for cattle to cross the Mauvais Pas, the animals were driven on to the glacier below and the surface had to be prepared for some distance with planks to bridge crevasses. Axes were used to level bumps in the ice and sometimes the cows were roped in case they fell into a slit.

Just beyond this point ignore a secondary right fork. Bear slightly left to the *Chapeau café* on a grassy knoll (1576 m.). Looking up the glacier you see the impressively prickly points of the Charmoz, Blaitière, Plan and Midi, while below are the last blue séracs of the glacier. 2 h. from Montenvers.

At the edge of the forest further down the path splits. The left branch is steep and rough for a short way and it passes close to the café at the Source de l'Arveyron and reaches the hamlet of Les Bois (see page 60). It is pleasanter to take the right fork through the woods to Le Lavancher village. There you join the main road between Chamonix and Argentière. Bus or train from Les Tines station rather lower down if required.

Pendant–Lognan traverse

In itself this is an enchanting walk which ends at Argentière in the upper part of the valley. It can be usefully combined with the previous excursion across the Mer de Glace, or started directly from Chamonix. Either way you may be tempted to use the lower stage of the Grands Montets cableway for descending, but this robs you of the best views of the Argentière glacier and its surrounding peaks. From Montenvers or Chamonix, about 5 h. to Argentière. For fuller information about Argentière and the Grands Montets cableway, see Section Three.

Setting out from the Montenvers, follow the previous route to the right fork which is ignored immediately above the Chapeau café. From Chamonix take a train or bus to Les Tines and Le Lavancher, then follow the well-marked path in the woods (keep right at a junction) to the *Chapeau*. 2 h.

The fork mentioned above is taken; a tortuous path climbs across the opening of the Chapeau stream to the north and into the forest; later join a large mule path coming up directly from Le Lavancher (the junction mentioned above). Chamonix starters can use the latter, which is easier, but you miss fine views of the Mer de Glace. The mule path crosses a pasture to the *Pendant chalets* (1778 m.); broad view of the valley below and of the Aigs. Rouges opposite. Now the path works round a rocky corner into the pretty flowered Chosalets forest which is traversed horizontally to open ground again. Continue over several streams draining from the snows above and a little further reach the *Croix de Lognan* (1975 m.), now the intermediate station of the Argentière–Grands Montets cableway; restaurant, shop, etc. Immediately above the station the path forks. Take the higher right-hand branch (the left-hand one is a shorter way down) and contour wide grassy slopes to the rock rib on which the old *Lognan hotel* stands (2032 m.). The hotel is closed. From this point you have a splendid view up and down the majestic *Argentière glacier*, with its main icefalls above and below. This is the second longest ice stream in the Mt. Blanc range, but the longest independent one because the Mer de Glace is fed by two other glaciers. The Argentière glacier is equally beautiful and reaches down to within 3 km. distance of its village. Altogether it is 9·5 km. long.

On the other side the glacier is overlooked by a huge mass of rock descending from the Aig. du Chardonnet, one of the most popular climbs in the district. 2 h. from the Chapeau.

Below the hotel descend a large mule path in zigzags to an open forest with rhododendron bushes; keep on the right side of a small stream and bear right to reach Argentière village and station along a jeep road. Or after a short way turn left down another jeep road, pass the cableway station and reach the main road (bus) at Les Chosalets village.

Montenvers–Jardin de Talèfre

Undoubtedly the oldest and most famous glacier walk for tourists in good training in the Alps. The object is to reach a large, sloping pear-shaped island, the Jardin, situated like an oasis in the circular glacier bowl of Talèfre. This bowl is a great reservoir of snow that contributes volume to one of the two main catchment basins feeding the Mer de Glace. Skirted by moraines and sparsely vegetated, the rocky island is contained by a perfect example of a glacier cirque. This in turn is rimmed by some of the most dramatic peaks in the Mt. Blanc range: the Moine, Verte, Droites, Courtes, Ravanel, Mummery, Triolet, etc. This 'garden midst eternal snows' owes its reputation to rare plants which might be found there, and for minerals you can see *en route*. A more lasting claim to fame is the strangely complete feeling of isolation it gives to the visitor; you are surrounded by unforgettable scenes of ice and rock and there is a classic view of Mt. Blanc in the background.

Magnificent in every way as this outing surely is, it should not be attempted by anyone unaccustomed to rough Alpine country, unless accompanied by a guide. By the standards of experienced mountain walkers this excursion is neither long nor difficult. The route up the middle of the Mer de Glace can be complicated by several groups of crevasses, and there are furiously rushing icy streams to negotiate on its surface. In one place there are several moulins (glacier mills), which are formed by circular water action. Further up, the rockface of Les Egralets is adorned with ladders (some vertical), iron stanchions and rails which could worry a person nervous of 'heights'. However, this is a well-trodden path leading to the *Couvercle hut* (restaurant/accommodation) (4 h.), from where an almost

horizontal traverse leads to the Jardin in another
30 min. Leave the Montenvers not later than seven in
the morning, to return comfortably in the afternoon.
See MB2, page 18.

Plan de l'Aiguille traverses

The main footpath across the Plan de L'Aiguille
terrace is described briefly and in the reverse direction
(Plan de l'Aiguille inn to Montenvers) on page 74.
This terrace is the most frequented half of a longer
traverse at a slightly higher level, beyond the Midi
cableway, to the Bossons glacier, from where you can
descend easily to the valley. The tall granite
battlements of the Aiguilles can be approached more
closely by climbing above the regular path to a higher
level and crossing two small easy glaciers, generally
without crevasses. After reaching the cableway you can
continue over the Pèlerins glacier to the Bossons
glacier, which can also be crossed to the top of the
Montagne de la Côte. This final section is only
recommended to experienced Alpine walkers. Stout
shoes or boots and spiked walking stick are advisable.
One of the most varied and rewarding excursions in
the region. The path is occasionally vague or non-
existent, so keep a sharp lookout for cairns.
Montenvers to cableway, 3 h. ; to Gare des Glaciers,
$3\frac{3}{4}$; to top of Montagne de la Côte, $4\frac{1}{2}$ h. From any
point on the walk allow 2 h. for descent to Chamonix.

From the Montenvers follow the pretty footpath
between larch and birch trees in the Plan de
L'Aiguille direction, with the main forest below. **Rise**
gradually and after rounding a corner (30 min.) the
path is joined by another from above, also coming
from the Montenvers at a higher level. Continue for
500 m. to a clearly marked fork. Climb left up this
small branch path over grassy slopes, gaining height
rapidly, towards stony slopes below the moraine of the
Nantillons glacier. The path is well marked till you
move right on to the moraine crest, then vague but
with many cairns. Go straight up, on the left side of
the glacier. There is an alternative line of cairns in a
little boulder valley to the left, below the moraine
crest. Reach large blocks where you work horizontally
right on to the glacier. Keep as high as possible and
endeavour to reach the glacier above a steep bare ice
slope (conditions vary). Arrive at the edge of a broad

CMB—E

plateau, snow or ice, stretching right across the glacier at 2500 m. Superb views of the Nantillons icefall above, ringed by the turrets and spires of the Charmoz, Grépon and Blaitière. $1\frac{3}{4}$ h.

Cross the glacier plateau horizontally south-west to the far side, then go up an unmistakable little path over the low dividing moraine to the other side. Descend a little and follow an intermittent track over rocks to the moraine of the *Blaitière glacier* (2475 m.). Keep within the broad line of marker cairns. Cross the Blaitière glacier on a line slanting somewhat *downwards*; the almost flat icefield is mainly stone-covered. On the other side cross more moraine (cairns) and find a small track leading slightly below the tiny Plan de l'Aiguille lake (2299 m.). In a few minutes reach a vague left fork, climbing back towards the lake. Follow this and bear sharp right away from the lake, working south round a little ridge and through a trough to join the path rising from the cableway station to the Pèlerins glacier. Large cairn, 2350 m. 3 h. from Montenvers.

All along this section there are wonderful savage scenes of bare brown rock and tumbling icefalls overhead, marking the faces of the Blaitière, Fou, Caiman, Crocodile and Plan peaks. Their names indicate the wild nature of the scenery. Finally an uninterrupted view of the Midi and Mt. Blanc bursts into sight. Below, the cableway station can be reached in a few minutes. Thus far, MB1, route nos. 166 and 167.

The next section, to the Gare des Glaciers (derelict cableway station), is the ordinary approach to the Grands Mulets hut, for climbing Mt. Blanc (MB1, route no. 8). Continue up the almost level path to a fork in a few minutes. Take the right branch leading on to the moraine (2385 m.) and descend briefly to the *Pèlerins glacier*. This is flat and you cross it horizontally to the far side where cairns mark the continuation track. The cableway passes directly overhead. The track crosses grass and rocks horizontally below the Aig. du Midi to the shell building of the *Gare des Glaciers* (2414 m.). $3\frac{3}{4}$ h. from Montenvers. Stupendous view of the contorted glacier junction of Bossons and Taconnaz straight ahead.

Most walkers will prefer to descend to Chamonix from here. A path goes down in the line of the ancient cableway, steep and rough at first to the *Pierre Pointue* rocks (2038 m.), then easier to the ancient *Para station* (1685 m.). Now go down a mule path beside the Creuse stream and finish at the bridge near the entrance to the Mt. Blanc tunnel.

Experienced walkers can continue for a short expedition on the Bossons glacier, at the actual base of Mt. Blanc. From the Gare des Glaciers follow the traverse path to the right which contours a stream bed, then rises gradually to the edge of the glacier. Pass a rock about 15 m. high called the *Pierre à l'Échelle*, where many years ago ladders were placed for parties to drag out on to the glacier if the crevasses were considered impassable. This short track also passes directly under a great gully some 200 m. wide, cleaving the wall of the Aig. du Midi. In the afternoon it is liable to discharge volleys of stones across the track, so it is not advisable to linger! The ground at the edge of the glacier is steep and loose; follow the cairns. If there is fresh snow on the glacier, or if the snow is very soft, do not attempt to cross it; turn back. In good conditions the glacier is bare ice and the position of crevasses can be seen well ahead. At this level a prominent terrace called the Plan Glacier, at about 2600 m., extends in a slightly rising half circle to the top of the Montagne de la Côte. The distance across the terrace is 1·5 km. Keep more or less in its centre, turning numerous crevasses, till you are above the last rock islands of the Côte. Then descend in the line of the islands to firm ground (2589 m.) and the site of *Balmat's bivouac* (2530 m.), an historically memorable spot. Directly above is the famous *Jonction*, where the Bossons and Taconnaz glaciers collide to form many crevasses and séracs, and behind this the rocks of the *Grands Mulets* with its fine new aluminium-clad hut.

It must be re-emphasised that the passage of the Bossons glacier can be very awkward for untrained persons, and even in good conditions the ice cataract can make intricate work of finding a safe route. Children should not be taken on this part of the glacier unless accompanied by an experienced climber.

From Balmat's bivouac a rough track twists downwards, round the point called Corbeau, to the Pyramides café (1895 m.). Further down is the Bossons chairlift.

Grands Mulets hut (3051 m.)

One of the two main starting points for climbing Mt. Blanc, frequently visited by tourists in company with guides or experienced mountaineers. Restaurant service and bunkhouse accommodation. Unqualified persons find their way to the hut without mishap, but this is more by luck than skill or judgement. The route is identical to the previous description except that you climb through the séracs of the Jonction above the Plan Glacier, and continue up crevassed slopes to the rocks on which the hut is perched. A splendid oasis surrounded by dazzling snowfields and icefalls. 3 h. from Plan de l'Aiguille cableway station (MB1, route no. 8).

Aiguilles Rouges traverses

Previously described under the Brévent and La Flégère are cross-slope walks between these cableways, and extensions in either direction. At this level on the mountain-side the complete excursion from Planpraz to the Col des Montets at the head of the Chamonix valley is known as the *Plan des Aiguilles Rouges traverse*. Most of it is now designated officially as part of the great Tour du Mt. Blanc trail, and the path is maintained and waymarked to standards laid down by the government. The traverse can be done comfortably in a day from Chamonix by first using the Brévent cableway to Planpraz, and at the far end by using a train or bus to return down the valley. All you need is a map. 4–5 h. walking, with unsurpassed views of the Mt. Blanc range.

Tougher walkers can find well-marked routes either on the crest of the Aigs. Rouges, or not far below it. The T.M.B. trail follows the ridge from the Bellachat inn over the Brévent summit to the Col du Brévent. The next section of ridge (for climbers only) is turned on the Chamonix side and you rejoin it at the Col du Lac Cornu. To continue it is now necessary to descend on the Diose side to the lake and make a big detour by the Lacs Noirs to recross the ridge at a pass of the same name. From there you descend to the Index cableway and so reach Lac Blanc, from where the ordinary traverse path is reached on the last leg to the road at the Col des Montets. 7–8 h.

Looking down on Chamonix from the Montenvers path

Conspicuous notices are posted on public footpaths if there is any danger for pedestrians. This one indicates the possibility of falling stones at a tempting fork

Montenvers train leaving Chamonix

Montenvers train in the forest

Scene through the motorman's window on the Montenvers railway.
Note the speed limit sign of 15 km./h.

Crossing a viaduct on the Montenvers railway

The restored 'Temple of Nature' near the Montenvers
Train arriving at the Montenvers (overleaf, above)
Scene at the Montenvers hotel (overleaf, below)

Terrace scene at the Montenvers hotel, with Mer de Glace and Grandes Jorasses behind

Grands Charmoz from path above the Montenvers

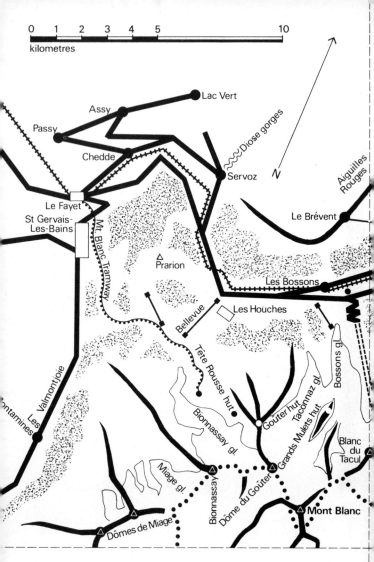

Chamonix Valley

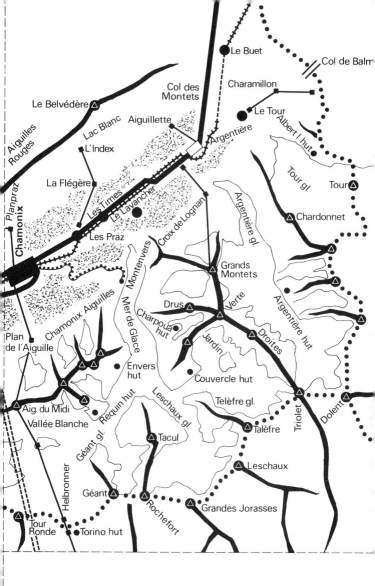

Clear signposts at a junction of paths near the Montenvers. Down to the left is the route to the Mer de Glace

The last few metres of the old equipped trail from the Montenvers hotel down to the moraine beside the Mer de Glace. The ladder has been replaced by a path cut in the rocks

Picnic party beside the Mer de Glace

Crevasses on the Mer de Glace. The ice is very rough and generally not slippery

The great west face of the Petit Dru, with the Aig. Verte behind

Last stage of the Brévent cableway, with Mt. Blanc and the Bossons glacier behind

Mer de Glace and Grandes Jorasses from near the Montenvers

Brévent cableway, with the summit snowfields and glaciers of Mt. Blanc

Upper stage of Aig. du Midi cableway. The Plan de l'Aiguille station and Chamonix valley are below, with the cableway crossing above the end of the Pèlerins glacier. (Opposite :) The Aiguilles Rouges

North face of the Aig. du Midi. The cableway lines are too fine to be seen in this picture, but they more or less rise parallel with the right-hand outline of the mountain. The peak immediately behind this outline is the Aig. du Goûter. Note the huge avalanche snow cloud pouring down the face of the mountain towards the glacier below. The covered bridge from the lower peak (cableway terminus) to the central peak can just be seen

Looking down into the Chamonix valley from the top station of the Aig. du Midi cableway. The inverted triangle of shadow on the opposite ridge is the Brévent

Looking down into the Chamonix valley, across the Pèlerins glacier, from the Midi–Plan ridge. Bossons glacier further left

Snow trail in the Vallée Blanche

*Grandes Jorasses (centre right) and Aig. du Géant (further right)
seen across the Vallée Blanche* (overleaf, above)

*Central gallery at the Aig. du Midi station, with the Drus, Verte,
Droites and Courtes in background* (overleaf, below)

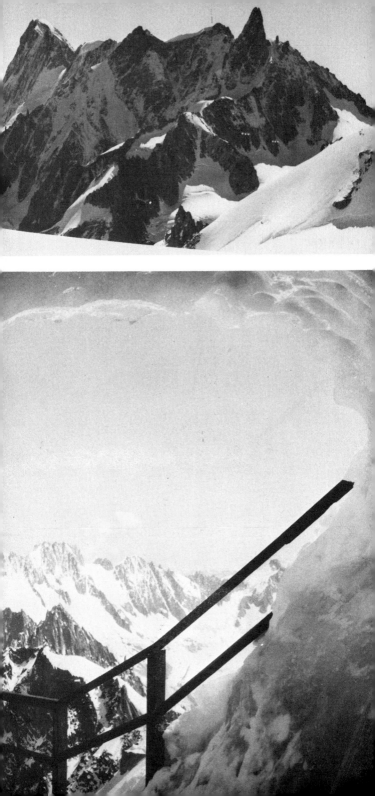

Mt. Blanc from the Midi–Géant cableway. The rock thumb on left is the famous and very difficult climb called the Grand Capucin. The rock fingers on the right are the Aigs. du Diable

The Tour Ronde and Géant glacier from the Midi–Géant cableway (overleaf)

Aig. du Géant and Géant glacier from the Midi–Géant cableway.
Note the trail on glacier in bottom right-hand corner

Mt. Blanc from the foot of the Aig. du Géant. Helbronner station is seen on the flat rock on left of picture, directly below the sharp rock peak of the Aig. Noire. A skitow can be seen on the snowfield to right of the station

Section two

Excursions from Les Houches

In the lower part of the valley *Les Houches* (population, 1200) is patronised both as a separate centre and as a starting point for excursions taken by people staying in Chamonix. The distance between the two is 7·5 km.; an hourly or more frequent bus service operates between Chamonix and Les Houches; the railway provides an additional service although the station is 10 min. walk from the village centre. There are six main hotels and as many pensions; also furnished apartments and campsites, shops, etc.

This is a picturesque modernised village straggling along its slip road above the River Arve for about 1 km., perfectly situated among sloping fields and certainly deserving the reputation for being the quietest holiday place in the valley.

Above the village, the best excursions on the south (Mt. Blanc) side of the valley are all linked with the Bellevue cableway; its terminus is at the west end of the main street. On the north side there are good paths winding up to the crest of the Aigs. Rouges.

5 North side of valley

Statue du Christ-Roi (1287 m.)

A gigantic work by G. Serraz (1934), situated on a rock near the hamlet of Le Coupeau on the north side of the valley. A side road over the river barrage just past Les Houches station in the Chamonix direction is taken in zigzags towards the hamlet. A signposted path on the right leads to a chapel and the statue (1 h. from Les Houches village, or 45 min. from station, on foot. Cars can be taken up the side road). Café nearby.

The statue and its pedestal are 20 m. high and weigh 200 tons. You can also see a bust of the famous alpinist, Pope Pius XI (Achille Ratti). Grand view of Mt. Blanc and the Aiguilles.

Merlet–Bellachat–Brévent

One of the grandest forest walks in the region, at a gentle gradient and shaded by an umbrella of great fir trees for a long way. An interesting combination is to ascend from Chamonix and descend to Les Houches. There are restaurants at the Merlet chalets and Bellachat.

From Les Houches station start along the road to the Statue du Christ-Roi and continue into the hamlet of Le Coupeau. Fork right (east) along a signposted path rising through the forest to a large clearing and the Merlet chalets (1562 m.) (2 h.). The path sidles into a wooded ravine where it is joined by another coming from Les Bossons and Chamonix. (This is the Henri Vallot traverse path which branches low down from the Chamonix–Plan Lachat–Bellachat walk, page 70.) You climb the left side of the stream bed and cross it higher up, then make a long rising traverse across the head of the forest and another ravine to the Bellachat inn (2151 m.) (2 h. from Merlet). Tremendous views of the main range all the way. Here you join the Chamonix route to the Brévent, up the left side of the Aigs. Rouges crest, to its summit in another 1½ h. Clear waymarks throughout. Downhill, you should be able to descend to Les Houches in half the time. This route is part of the T.M.B. trail.

Gorges de la Diose (Diosaz)

The alternative spelling is the older form; it has been changed on recent maps to the phonetic pronunciation. The main gorge is a few minutes walk from Servoz village, below Les Houches. Bus service. The gorge carries the stream emptying from the wild valley which flanks the opposite (west) side of the Aigs. Rouges range. There are no recognised footpaths in the lower part of this valley, which is noted for ferrous ores embedded in its rocks, while the upper part is traversed by cross-country routes to the town of Sixt further north. Therefore the gorge itself has been developed as one of the most popular tourist attractions in the neighbourhood by means of an artificial 'path' suspended above its raging waters.

A good path leads to the entrance (admission fee); restaurant, shop, etc. Inside the deep narrow cleft, which has sheer vegetated rock walls, the path goes up to a catwalk and gallery fixed to the walls. It works up one side, then crosses to the other, about 30 m. above the stream, and enables the most striking parts of the gorge to be seen in 20 min. There are seven small consecutive waterfalls. At the upper end you reach another branch of the system called the Soufflet, where the sky is almost shut out; higher up the chasm is spanned by an enormous rock forming a natural bridge. Trout caught in the stream are served as a delicacy at the restaurant, but there seems to be no trace of the once famous lobsters which used to abound among the rocks.

At the entrance to the gorge there is a striking view of the limestone precipices of the Rochers des Fiz to the north. In this direction there is an excellent footpath from Servoz village (road to above the hamlet of Le Mont) to *Lac Verte* near the base of the remains of a vast landslide, called Le Dérochoir, where in 1751 something like a hundred million tons of cliff are said to have fallen down from the west side of the Rochers des Fiz. The fall filled the valley with such a dust cloud that it was rumoured a volcanic outburst had taken place. A small track, sometimes exposed to stonefall, slants across the upper edge of the landslide to a gap in the ridge above, called the Passage du Dérochoir (2230 m.). This leads to the famous limestone waste of the *Désert de Platé*, a wilderness resembling a petrified glacier, rich in fossils and geologically fascinating. 2 h. on foot to the lake—mirrored view of Mt. Blanc on its surface; or 1 h. by using a car up to the roadhead.

6 South side of valley

Bellevue cableway (Col de Vose or Vosa) (1790 m.)
Rising directly from Les Houches village to the ridge dividing the Chamonix valley from St. Gervais is one of the most useful mechanical mountaineers in the region. This cableway was built as long ago as 1936, and the service equipment has been constantly improved, so that the journey which originally took 12 min. is now done in 4 min. As a cableway it is one of the least spectacular in the region. Its value lies in the provision of cheap transport to one of the finest viewpoints in the area. The profiles of the Mt. Blanc range are quite different from those seen from the Brévent and Aig. du Midi. The cableway carries a great deal of traffic, and many climbers from Chamonix start this way for climbing Mt. Blanc by the St. Gervais Route. The terminus is situated on a grassy saddle in a glorious spot with wide open spaces of pasture on all sides. At the top station there is a buffet, and the line of the Mt. Blanc Tramway is seen a short distance down on the other side of the broad ridge. The cableway terminus is situated midway between two stations on the railway.

A few minutes along the path to the west you arrive at the *Bellevue hotel* (1786 m.) and a railway halt (not a proper boarding place for trains); this is in the downward direction of the line. Further down still, alongside the tracks, you reach the actual saddle of the *Col de Vose* (1653 m.). Hotel, shop and railway station; all told about 20 min. walk from cableway. Here you find a chairlift going up to the *Prarion hotel* (1853 m.); telescopes and viewfinder (on foot, 30 min.). The grassy headland of the *Prarion summit* (1967 m.) is merely 20 min. away and is an obligatory walk.

The total panorama from any point between the cableway and the Prarion is of the finest order. Looking towards Mt. Blanc, its summit is concealed by the dark bank of cliffs of the Aig. du Goûter. In contrast, to the right the northern ice precipices of the Aig. de Bionnassay sparkle brightly and fall into the snaking Bionnassay glacier below. To the left stands the majestic Mt. Blanc du Tacul followed by all the Chamonix Aiguilles; behind them, the Verte, Chardonnet and Tour. A perfect view is gained of the entire length of the Chamonix valley up to the Col de Balme and Col des Montets, enclosed by the long serrated ridge of the Aigs. Rouges, from the Buet to the Brévent and Gorges de la Diose. From the Prarion you get a better view of the escarpment landscape of limestone cliffs and peaks to the north and west.

Easy paths, hardly rising or falling, criss-cross the pastures of the Col de Vose, and all this ground provides splendid ski-runs in winter.

A walk down to St. Gervais takes 2 h. and can be varied. Frequent trains and buses for returning to the Chamonix valley.

Mt. Blanc Tramway (2386 m.)
This rack-and-pinion railway starts at Le Fayet and has stations on the way up at St. Gervais and the Col de Vose before it passes the Bellevue cableway. From Chamonix and Les Houches the railway is invariably joined at the top of the cableway. To board the train you must either walk down the line to the Col de Vose (15–20 min.) or walk up to the Col du Mt. Lachat (20 min.). In fact many visitors using the cableway prefer to walk along the line all the way to its terminus (45 min.).

The carriages were originally drawn by steam engines (1909). The entire line was electrified by overhead pick-up and new coaches brought into

service in 1956. The journey from Le Fayet to the top
station takes under an hour, and only 15 min. from
the Col de Vose. After the latter station is the *Col du
Mt. Lachat halt* (2073 m.), which is not a place that
anyone would alight at; the only reason for its
existence seems to be where two trains can pass in
opposite directions. Less than $1\frac{1}{2}$ km. further the train
enters a short tunnel, followed immediately by the
terminus station at the *Nid d'Aigle* rocks (2386 m.),
in sight of the Bionnassay glacier; restaurant. 12·8 km.
from Le Fayet.

You are greeted by a most wonderful view of the
Aig. de Bionnassay, one of the most independent and
beautiful satellites of Mt. Blanc. Its northern face is
crumpled by magnificent ice cliffs overlooking the
glacier. Directly above the restaurant the corrugated
cliffs of the Aig. du Goûter are seen in a
foreshortened view.

Leading away from the station is a small track
crossing barren ground to the edge of the glacier
(20 min.). In no circumstances should you venture
on the ice, which at this point is riddled with crevasses
and séracs. Opposite these are the dark precipices of
the Arête du Tricot, a scene of avalanches and
stonefall.

Tête Rousse chalet-hotel (3167 m.)
One of the few mountain huts owned by the C.A.F.
in the Mt. Blanc range that can be reached easily and
safely by tourists or mountain walkers. For a day trip,
it is the principal object of most visitors who travel on
the Bellevue cableway and Mt. Blanc Tramway. The
path is stony and rough all the way but at a reasonable
gradient, clearly marked and without danger. Highly
recommended. The walk is the first stage for climbing
Mt. Blanc by the St. Gervais Route. Refreshments and
meals at the chalet; bunkhouse accommodation. 3 h.
or less from Tramway terminus at Nid d'Aigle (MB1,
route no. 5).

From the Tramway station go along the path towards
the glacier for a short way, then branch sharp left and
climb zigzags in a stony hollow enclosed on the left by
cliffs. The track is perfectly clear up to a boulder field
and broken-down cabin called the Rognes at the top
(2685 m.). Occasionally chamois have been sighted on
nearby rocks, but in common with the rest of the

Mt. Blanc range these graceful animals seem to have disappeared from this part of the Alps.

Now turn right (south-east) and cross a stonefield (cairns) to the foot of a broken rock ridge, up which the path winds in many zigzags to a snowy headland at the top (3132 m.). You see the chalet on the right, across a snowfield. Follow a trail in the snow and so reach the rocks on which the building stands.

By walking a few metres to the south you can look over a precipitous drop and the crevasse-slashed surface of the Bionnassay glacier is at your feet. The snowfield trail can generally be clearly seen leading up to the ribs and gullies that seam the face of the Aig. du Goûter, up which the route goes to the Goûter hut (in sight) at the top of the cliffs, from where the actual summit of Mt. Blanc is gained. The face of the Aig. du Goûter is notorious for bad rock and stonefall, and competent mountaineering parties normally only climb it in the early morning or evening.

Train on the Mt. Blanc tramway

Aig. de Bionnassay and its glacier from the Col de Vose, beside the Mt. Blanc tramway and Bellevue cableway

Spring skiing on the Col de Vose

Section three

Excursions from Argentière

Rather more than 8 km. from Chamonix and near the head of the valley the road and railway reach *Argentière* (1252 m.). Unlike Les Houches, all traffic leaving and entering Chamonix from Switzerland passes through this village (population, 500), which is consequently always busy. More so too than Les Houches, Argentière attracts a wider range of holiday interests, for it is an ideal base for exploring the northern end of the Mt. Blanc range and for easy walking days across a grassy ridge marking the frontier between France and Switzerland.

The village owns to five main hotels, numerous pensions and apartment houses, and several campsites. All main services with good if small shops ; combined tourist office and guides' bureau. The train journey from Chamonix takes 17 min. ; 25 min. by bus, calling at cableway stations in the valley.

Argentière is an uncluttered village and its great glacier once descended almost to the houses. It has now retreated some way up, leaving an open plain of stones and pebbles in which shrubbery and trees grow profusely. This zone, to the immediate east of the village, is combed by paths and there are many pleasant picnic glades.

Three cableway systems are associated with the village, among them the second highest and most recently constructed téléphérique in the region—the Croix de Lognan–Grands Montets line. The other two are the Aiguillette or Béchar chairlift and the combined Charamillon–Col de Balme chairlifts and télécabine. The latter system starts from the village of Le Tour, further up the valley. There are more skilifts in evidence here than in any other part of the valley. In winter the slopes of the Col de Balme and Lognan are ideal for beginners.

Information concerning short walks is appended to the main excursions described below.

To reach *Le Tour* village the train can be taken to the next station up the line, at *Montroc* (2·2 km.). Here the valley divides : one branch goes up in 20 min. on foot to Le Tour (good road, buses), the Col de Balme (bridlepath and cableways) and walking routes to the Swiss resort of Trient across the frontier ; the other over the Col des Montets (1461 m.) which carries the main road to Vallorcine and the Swiss frontier. On the other side the road descends to Le Châtelard (fork right to Trient) and Martigny. The railway passes through a tunnel, 1·9 km. long, under the road col and emerges at the Buet village not far from Vallorcine. The line ends at Martigny. This is the only railway tunnel in France provided with a pedestrian sidewalk, because in winter there is an avalanche danger for persons on foot who wish to cross the Col des Montets from Argentière to Vallorcine.

When you leave the station at Montroc, turn left, cross the River Arve and bear right up the road to Le Tour (1462 m.).

Trains and buses in combination produce a situation where no one need wait longer than 30 min. for transport in the valley between Chamonix–Argentière–Montroc–Le Tour and intermediate cableways. The early-morning trains and buses from Chamonix in the Argentière direction are always crowded on a fine day and you are advised to reach the departure stations early to get a seat. A seat on the right-hand side of the coach, facing up the valley, is best for views.

7 Cableways

Croix de Lognan–Grands Montets cableway (3271 m.)
A modern fast téléphérique, opened in 1963. The journey takes only 15 min. to rise through a vertical interval of 2030 m., including changing at the half-way station. Buses call at the departure station, situated 1 km. below Argentière in the Chamonix direction. Huge carpark.

From Argentière station cross the railway bridge over the Arve and on the right descend an embankment by a path which soon forks right. Follow the path over a bridge (stream) to a larger bridge over the main stream coming from the Argentière glacier. Continue in the same direction (south-west) and join a road a few steps from cableway station (10 min.). Cars should turn off the main road at *Les Chosalets* hamlet, where the road makes a 90° bend over a bridge (River Arve). The access road runs along the river bank to cableway.

The *Croix de Lognan* and mid-way station (1972 m.) are found on a delightful pasture below some old chalets. Large restaurant and shop; crèche for young children in winter. Most recommendable for those who do not ride down to the valley is the easy walk along the big traverse path to the old *Lognan inn*

(2032 m.), with its splendid views of the Argentière glacier, followed by the descent on foot by mule path to Argentière (2 h. all told). The traverse path can be taken in the opposite direction, along pretty forest trails by the Pendants chalets to the Chapeau café and Mer de Glace, or to Le Lavancher and Chamonix (2–3 h.). These walks are described on page 81.

While riding on the upper stage of the line it is soon possible to see over the top of the Aigs. Rouges behind and a most wonderful scene of interlocking ranges unfolds to the north and west. The top station is situated 26 m. below the summit of the *Aig. des Grands Montets* (3297 m.). In days gone by this mountain was considered one of the essential training climbs for alpinists. The summit is reached by an equipped footpath; ice possible after bad weather. Snack-bar. The Grands Montets is the last eminence in the Aig. Verte chain of peaks, before it plunges into the Chamonix valley. This sub-range is one of the finest spurs in the greater Mt. Blanc range, and its rock climbs and ice routes are among the hardest in the Alps.

Warnings addressed to ill-equipped or inexperienced persons are displayed concerning the adjoining snowfields. These are extensive, partly crevassed (badly so as a rule on the east side of the mountain) and fairly steep in places. Short access paths have been cut in the rocks that reach them, for summer skiing and climbing. The popular slope for both rises behind the mountain, south-eastwards towards the *Petit Aig. Verte* (3508 m.); in mid-season there is a large trail up this peak, about 1 h. distant (MB2, route no. 106).

It need hardly be said that the Grands Montets is a magnificent viewpoint. The panorama of great peaks at the north end of the range is all-embracing and the nearness to stupendous faces of rock and ice makes a lasting impression. Laid out like a map you can chart the courses of the Mer de Glace and Argentière glaciers on either hand; the first is wrinkled like elephant skin, the other is like a sheet of white satin. The great Argentière glacier is enclosed by varied glaciated peaks—the Chardonnet, Argentière, Tour Noir, while Mt. Dolent is clearly seen at its head where the boundaries of France, Italy and Switzerland meet. The Aig. Verte, monarch of the sub-range, rises elegantly overhead; you have glimpses of its immense

145

wall—over 1000 m. high and extended by the Droites and Courtes—which borders the south side of the Argentière glacier. Towards the Mer de Glace the bold double summit of the Drus rises behind an intervening ridge, and beyond you see the Chamonix Aiguilles and Mt. Blanc.

To benefit from the excellent facilities at the Grands Montets for practice climbing on rock and ice you should enrol at the bureaux in Chamonix or Argentière. The descent of the crevassed snowfields and glacier lying on the east side of the mountain to the Argentière glacier is a short cut to the Argentière hut (2 h.), and should only be done by competent roped parties. Competent parties can also descend easily below the ski slopes to the Mer de Glace and Montenvers.

Aiguillette chairlift (1727 m.)
The chairlift swings through forest on the Aigs. Rouges slope directly above Argentière. The departure station is situated on the left side of the main road as you leave the village in the Montroc and Col des Montets direction. The top station is a few steps from the Plan des Aigs. Rouges traverse path which runs at about this level all the way down to Chamonix and beyond. A lower path to the south crosses a flowered glade behind a rock called the *Béchar* (practice climbs) from where you can descend in the forest to Argentière in 1 h. or less. Equally short and pleasant, a path to the north can be followed down to the Trélechamp hamlet on the main road below the Col des Montets.

Opposite the cableway café you have an end-on view up the Argentière glacier to Mt. Dolent at the top. To the left is the Tour glacier and its pyramid peak; to the right the soaring snow cap of the Aig. Verte, and, as always, down the valley the mighty mass of Mt. Blanc dominates the scene.

To join the upper level of the Plan des Aigs. Rouges traverse path, follow a track uphill (west), then south-west across scrub and rocks to a barrier of cliffs. The track goes up this vaguely and steeply. You pass the *Aiguillette*, a rock pinnacle about 20 m. high which is used for practice climbing (quite difficult); the track follows a gully before continuing to slant over the stony mountain-side to another gully (zigzags) which emerges on a hummocky plateau containing the *Chésery lakes*. Exceptionally fine views. 1 h. In another

146

hour you can reach Lac Blanc (page 77) along a good track to the west. Stout shoes or boots will be needed for comfort on these walks.

Connections for walkers between the cableways of the Aiguillette, La Flégère/Index and Planpraz/ Brévent (q.v.) will be evident from routes described earlier.

Le Tour–Charamillon–Col de Balme cableways (2186 m.)
For Le Tour, if you start on foot from Argentière, a longer but pleasant walk can be taken on the east side of the valley, to avoid the main road. At the north end of the village turn right along a road across the river ; turn left and pass the church on this side, keeping to an unmade road near the river. In a short distance a path branches right across fields to the railway. Cross to the other side by an underground passageway and climb a zigzag in a wood to the road and hotel at *Le Planet*. At the first bend in this road (north) take a path to the right and climb gradually along the top of a wood to join a higher path. Continue by descending towards Montroc. At the bottom do not cross the bridge into this hamlet. Continue along a path beside fields till you can turn left and enter *Le Tour* village. 1 h. Bus service, or access by good road from Montroc station.

The first stage of the chairlift starts from the top end of the village. At a height of only a few metres above the ground, the chairs go up broad pastures to the *Charamillon chalets* (1850 m.) in 8 min. The footpath to the same place is close by. 1 h. Inn and restaurant.

The second stage, chairlift and télécabine, does not actually reach the Col de Balme. It slants further right and ends some distance below the frontier ridge but at about the same height as the col to the north (2191 m.). 8 min. A good traverse path leads to the col in 15 min. The footpath from Charamillon to the col climbs at an easy angle directly to the col over bare slopes of grass and black slaty debris. 1 h. Hotel-restaurant on Swiss side.

The view is tremendous. You see the Mt. Blanc range from the Aig. du Chardonnet on the immediate left to the Aig. du Goûter at the bottom of the Chamonix valley. Looking north into Switzerland the Bernese Alps are prominent and culminate on the right in the Jungfrau, Mönch and Bietschhorn. A better view is obtained by climbing a path above the col to the *Tête de la Balme* (2321 m.) (15 min.). This can be extended to the crumbling rock peak of the *Croix de Fer* (2343 m.) in Swiss territory (30 min.).

A fairly steep track leads down to Trient on the Swiss side of the pass, where the main road is joined (1½ h.) and buses are found for returning over the Col des Montets to Argentière.

Albert Premier hut (2702 m.)

One of the most recommendable excursions in the Chamonix region, with an excellent footpath at an easy angle from the top of the Col de Balme cableway. Take the traverse path in the opposite direction to the col, facing towards the Chamonix valley. After a while the path drops a little to the Charamillon lake, then rises progressively to a corner in the Bec de Picheu ridge. Here you get a wonderful view of the Tour glacier. Round the corner the trail becomes quite rocky and it eventually joins the moraine beside the glacier. The moraine leads to the fine new hut which belongs to the C.A.F. Restaurant and bunkhouse accommodation. 2 h. from cableway. The hut is named after Albert I, King of the Belgians, who provided through the Belgian Alpine Club funds for the original building. He died in a climbing accident on practice rocks in Belgium in 1934.

From the hut you can almost see into the entire upper snowfield and basin of the Tour glacier, which is broad rather than long. On the left is the popular climb of the Aig. du Tour, on the right the superb snow peak of the Aig. du Chardonnet. Inexperienced persons are not advised to wander on to the glacier, reached in a few minutes along a small track. While the slopes are not particularly steep there are many crevasses, generally not very evident and often masked by fresh coverings of snow.

Taking the path all the way down to Le Tour is also recommended. Fork left below the Charamillon lake (i.e. ignore cableway path to right) and join the Col de Balme path at the Charamillon chalets. 2 h. to Le Tour (MB2, route no. 6).

Cascade de Bérard

The most attractive waterfall in the Argentière neighbourhood. Go to the Buet station (road or rail) on the north side of the Col des Montets. Take the small road beside the Buet hotel, going to the Poya hamlet, at the entrance to the Eau de Bérard valley. Continue by a good path to the waterfall where huge rocks are jammed in a miniature ravine (20 min. from station). A nearby cave is said to be the den of forgers who produced counterfeit money over 200 years ago.

At the top of this valley is Le Buet (3094 m.), one of the classical viewpoints of the Alps, and generally regarded as providing the finest panorama—end to end—of the Mt. Blanc range. The mountain was climbed by Bourrit (second ascent) in 1775. The climb—for which there is an overnight chalet near the head of the valley—is only suitable for experienced mountain walkers.

Cableway to La Flégère, with Chamonix below and the Aig. du Midi and Mt. Blanc in background (left)

Heavy snowfall covering the Drus, seen from the Montenvers footpath

Séracs above the Mer de Glace

Small moraine lake on the Chapeau path, with Grandes Jorasses and Aig. du Tacul behind (overleaf, left)

Half-way up the Mer de Glace, with views of Mt. Mallet and the Aig. du Géant

Walking party on the Mer de Glace, showing the Géant icefall to the right and the Aig. du Géant up to the left

North face of the Grandes Jorasses, from path to the Couvercle and the Jardin

Mt. Blanc from the Couvercle, one of the classic views in the range.
The Géant icefall and glacier are in the centre, Vallée Blanche further
right, and the rock peak of the Requin on far right

Grazing herds are a common sight on all mountain pastures in summer. These grazing grounds are the true 'alps', a name often mistakenly given to the mountains above them

Scene on the footpath from the Montenvers to Plan de l'Aiguille. Left to right : the Blaitière, with Nantillons glacier below ; the Caïmen and Crocodile, overtopped by the little pinnacled summit of the Aig. du Plan, with its steep glacier flowing below. Further right : the descending staircase of rock peaks called the Deux Aigles, Pèlerins and Peigne (overleaf, left)

Aig. du Midi from the Plan de l'Aiguille footpath (above)

Mt. Blanc and Mer de Glace basin from near the Grands Montets (above right)

Mt. Blanc and the Chamonix Aiguilles (Mer de Glace face) from near the Grands Montets (below right)

Mt. Blanc and the Chamonix Aiguilles rising above a sea of cloud, from near the Grands Montets station

On the moraine of the Nantillons glacier, from the little path leading to the glacier. Aig. de Blaitière above (overleaf, left)

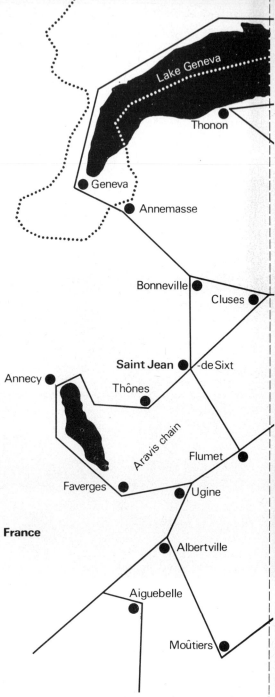

Road routes for touring by car or coach

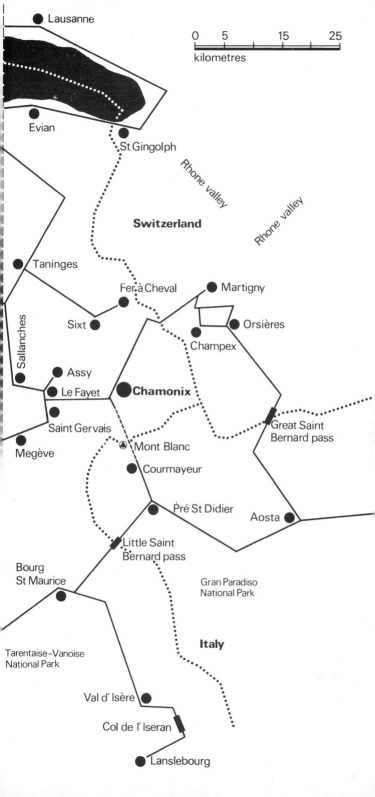

Section four

Touring by car and coach

It cannot be stated too strongly that the infinite possibilities for day trips by car from Chamonix are without equal for interest and variety. Painted on a vast canvas, the changing scenes and landscapes of lakes, valleys and mountains add to rather than detract from the merit of making Chamonix the base for a holiday. A selection of some of the best tours is described in the following pages, but anyone capable of reading a large-scale road map of Chamonix and its surrounds for say 100 km. in any direction will have no difficulty inventing and exploring many alternatives.

For touring by car or coach some points to watch are: (1) Passports are required for even the shortest journeys across a frontier. It is advisable to inquire about restrictions on the importation and export of goods before starting out. (2) When crossing frontiers a less favourable rate of exchange may be given at booths near customs houses than in banks in towns. For day excursions there is a good case for buying small amounts of foreign currency in Chamonix before leaving. (3) The price of petrol (gasoline) varies considerably between France, Italy and Switzerland. In 1968, for instance, petrol coupons were available for tourists visiting Italy, so affording a reduction of 25%. The procedure for obtaining these coupons is simplified by making the necessary arrangements at home, before going on holiday.

Car drivers with little experience of driving on Alpine roads should always consider returning before nightfall. On the whole all roads are good, but many sections on the best tours are narrow, winding, steep and with a sheer drop on one side or the other. Plenty of garages will be found as well as places to pull off the road for a halt. Petrol consumption tends to be high because of low-gear work; despite this gradients rarely exceed 1 in 8.

8 Short journeys

Gorges de la Diose (*Servoz*)

See page 132. Leave Chamonix by the old main road in the Le Fayet direction, drive to Les Bossons (glacier on left) and join the new motor road before passing Les Houches railway station on the right. Cross the Arve by the Sainte-Marie bridge and continue to the next right fork. Reach Servoz village by this road along the right bank of the Arve. 20 min.

Assy chapel and Lac Vert

See pages 16 and 133. Take the road to Servoz as for the Gorges de la Diose, then continue along the old Chamonix–Le Fayet road, above the right bank of the Arve. You climb, then descend with numerous bends to La Motte. From here a steep zigzag road forking right climbs directly to Assy. The longer and better road descends to Passy before climbing in many wide zigzags to the plateau of Assy. 45 min. A feast of modern art and Roman inscriptions.

A narrow road continues east through a magnificent pine forest to Lac Vert. A walk round the lake has been described as the most romantic experience in the region. 15 min. (1 h. from Chamonix). Impressive views of Mt. Blanc range all the way after Servoz.

Courmayeur and Aosta

From Chamonix take the bypass road (Route Blanche) circling round the railway station (no direct access from railway station itself) and continue to the sharp left turn of the access road rising in easy zigzags to the tunnel. In front of the tunnel enter the lane indicated. Toll charge according to engine capacity of vehicle (see page 46). Maintain a speed of about 60 km./h. through tunnel and do not overtake other vehicles. Customs inspection at Italian end. A fast motor road leads down to Courmayeur, which is reached by one of two slip roads on left. The main road continues down into the magnificent Aosta valley whose sides are clothed in vineyards, and you pass several of its famous castles, all of which can be visited. Superb views of sharp snowy peaks in the Gran Paradiso National Park on right, and behind you there is always a tremendous view of the Italian (Courmayeur) side of Mt. Blanc. Reach *Aosta* (fork left from bypass round town) in 45 min. from Courmayeur; this old walled town is exceedingly picturesque, with many fine buildings, and is the best shopping centre in the region. Return by same route.

9 Day excursions

Cols des Aravis and de la Colombière

A circuit through grand limestone country to the west of the Chamonix valley. Take the main road down the valley to Le Fayet, then turn left up to St. Gervais-les-Bains. At the top of the town fork right along the Megève road, overlooked by *Mt. d'Arbois* and *Mt. Joly* (cableways) to the left. *Megève* is a famous winter sports centre. Continue along R.N. 212 to *Praz-sur-Arly* and into the upper entrance of the Arly gorge, deep and verdant. At the village of *Flumet* turn right and follow R.N. 509 across the *Arondine gorges* to *La Giettaz* and the *Col des Aravis* (1498 m.); enchanting view across the famous limestone escarpments of the district, with Mt. Blanc behind. The road descends in zigzags to *La Clusaz* and *St. Jean-de-Sixt*. Turn right into the Chinaillon valley, up through *Grand-Bornand* along D.4 towards the *Col de la Colombière*; splendid views of the barren limestone range of the Aravis. The col (1618 m.) provides a superb panorama of the district, with its culminating peak of *Pointe Percée* (2752 m.) to the right. The road descends the Foron valley to *Le Reposoir*, a Carthusian monastery near the village of *Pralong*. The building dates from 1151. At this point you can see the opening in the summit of Pointe Percée, hence its name, through which daylight penetrates and at certain hours the sun or moon can be seen shining. At the bottom you reach *Cluses* in the Arve valley. Return by the main road R.N. 506 (R.N. 202) to *Sallanches* and *Le Fayet*. Round trip from Chamonix, 120 km.

Sixt and Fer à Cheval
A magnificent venue, one of the most attractive scenes in the Alps. Take the main road down the valley to Le Fayet. Continue in the main valley to *Sallanches*. On the left, Pointe Percée (2752 m.), the highest mountain in the limestone escarpment chain of the Aravis, with which the name of the famous Swiss climber F. Genecand is associated, who under the name of Tricouni invented nails for boots which gained world-wide acceptance; on the right the Aig. de Varan (2541 m.). Just below Sallanches, on the right, you have a clear view of the *Arpennaz waterfall*, 200 m. high. Follow the main road past interesting caves in the precipices of the Rochers de Balme above, to *Cluses*. Turn right along the road crossing the short *Col de Châtillon* (740 m.) and descend to *Taninges* in the *Giffre valley*. Keep right along the road up this valley, R.N. 507, to *Samoëns*, a quiet summer resort. The valley narrows and you drive through the Tines gorges to *Sixt*. This is the main tourist centre in the valley. 17th-century buildings. In a few more kilometres you reach the roadhead at the top of the

valley at the *Plan du Lac*, restaurant (950 m.). 110 km.
from Chamonix, return by same route.

The valley is enclosed by one of the finest examples
of a limestone cirque (amphitheatre) to be seen in
Europe. The floor is girt with beech woods while the
semi-circle of cliffs has an entirely inaccessible
appearance. They are overlooked by higher peaks of
rock and snow. The highest point is to the left, the
Pic de Tenneverge (2985 m.). Its precipices rise in a
series of remarkable tiers for 2000 m., imparting an
enormous scale to the scene. A series of seven
waterfalls descends the face of the precipice, about
500 m. high, and one of them shoots out of a hole in
a blank wall. Long ago mines were worked on these
heights; strange to relate, Jacques Balmat, the
conqueror of Mt. Blanc, lost his life at the age of
72 (1834) while seeking for gold in the glen leading
up to the mountains on the left. However, another
story relates that he was murdered by adversaries.

Footpaths lead to the base of the waterfalls, though
care must be taken on approaching them too closely
because of possible stonefall. A detailed guidebook
for walkers and climbers has been published recently
for this district, which includes the Fer à Cheval
(*Dents du Midi Region*, West Col Productions).

Geneva and its lake
By the main road through Le Fayet, Sallanches,
Bonneville and Annemasse, Geneva is 86 km. from
Chamonix. A beautiful city with fine buildings and
thoroughfares, and a major European centre for
international, political, commercial and welfare
organisations. Places of interest include: Parks—Mon
Repos, Perle du Lac, Grange and Eaux-Vives.
Buildings—Palais des Nations, Ariana museum,
Art museum, Monument de la Réformation, Town
Hall, St. Pierre cathedral.

A long circular tour round the shores of the lake is
feasible in a day from Chamonix. On the way to
Geneva turn right at *Cluses* and follow R.N. 202 to
Taninges, *Les Gets* (col) and *Thonon-les-Bains* on the
south shore of the lake. Drive along the lakeside to
Evian and *St. Gingolph* at the foot of the Grammont;
Swiss frontier. The road turns inland to cross the
broad delta of the Rhône before turning north along
the Swiss shore through *Villeneuve*, *Montreux* (Château
de Chillon and famous view of Dents du Midi at east

end of lake), *Vevey* and so to *Lausanne* above the lake.
These are all splendid resorts in the grand style and
in a situation comparable with the French Riviera. The
lakeside road continues through Morges, Rolle and
Nyon to *Geneva*. Keep a sharp lookout for road signs
in Lausanne and Geneva, which have complicated
one-way traffic systems. There is a new fast motorway
further inland between Lausanne and Geneva, if you
wish to make up time. Return to Chamonix by
Annemasse and Bonneville. The round trip is
about 300 km.

Annecy and its lake
This is probably the most popular lakeside resort in
France. The journey can be made direct by fairly fast
roads through *Bonneville* and *La Roche-sur-Foron*
(110 km.). More recommendable are scenic routes
through the mountains, which are not much longer.
Go out by one route and return by the other.

    1. From Chamonix follow the Col des Aravis drive
to *Flumet*. Instead of turning right up the road to the
col, continue straight ahead and descend the enclosed
wooded Arly gorges to *Ugine*, a small industrial town.
Here you join R.N. 508 to *Faverges* and the south end
of the lake. The road takes the west shore through
Duingt and *Sevrier* to Annecy. 120 km.

    2. Follow the Col des Aravis route over this pass to
St. Jean–de-Sixt, then turn left on R.N. 509 and
continue by this road to *Thônes*, *Morette* and the
lakeside at *Veyrier*, on the east shore. The road
continues prettily on this side to Annecy. 130 km.

    Annecy is a town of great antiquity, built on a series
of complex streams, and with narrow streets in the
old quarter, 16th-century churches and a famous
château, open to the public. Splendid walks beside
the lake.

Col de l'Iseran circuit
A long drive through magnificent scenery of the
Graian Alps. The col is the highest metalled road
pass in the Alps. Start as for the first alternative to
Annecy, and reach *Ugine*. From here take R.N. 212 to
Albertville in the Isère valley. This valley is followed
all the way to the col. The road (R.N. 90) is fast to
Moûtiers-Salins, after which it winds in a narrow defile
to *Bourg St. Maurice*. A short distance outside this
town the road is joined at *Séez village* by the route

across the Little St. Bernard pass from Italy. Crossing this pass provides a shorter way from Chamonix: go through the tunnel, pass Courmayeur and soon turn right off the Aosta road to *Pré St. Didier*. Behind this village a good road over the *Little St. Bernard* climbs in many zigzags and you enter France again at the top (2188 m.). The scenery is outstanding; superb views of Mt. Pourri and other high glaciated peaks in the Tarentaise massif of the Graian Alps. The descent to Séez is comfortable, with zigzags to finish.

The upper valley is densely forested to the *Tignes barrage*, a large artificial lake contoured by the road on the east side and through a number of tunnels. You enter a wide meadow and reach *Val d'Isère* (cableways), one of the premier winter resorts in France, at an altitude of 1800 m.; quiet and pleasant in summer and noted for first-rate walking country. A few kilometres further the impressive climb to the *Col de L'Iseran* commences, many zigzags and a road surface which is generally good. At the top (2769 m.) you find an hotel and restaurant in a bleak spot, with tremendous views down the Isère valley and of its surrounding peaks which include Mt. Pourri (3779 m.), Grande Sassière (3747 m.) and the Tsanteleina (3605 m.), while the deep trench of the Arc valley and Haute Maurienne awaits you on the other side. At the bottom of the steep descent the road bypasses the villages of *Bonneval-sur-Arc* and *Bessans* and you reach *Lanslevillard* and *Lanslebourg* at a junction with the road over the Col du Mont Cenis. Bessans and Lanslebourg were destroyed in reprisals by the Germans in 1944 and reconstruction work is still in progress. Along this section you can see many religious monuments erected by pilgrims journeying to Rome over the centuries. Continue down the valley past old fortresses perched on cliffs above the River Arc to the fortified town of *Modane*, at the entrance to the Mont–Cenis railway tunnel. The old town is picturesque and great forests cover the mountain-sides on all sides. The lower Maurienne valley, through *St. Michel* and *St. Jean*, has a fast road, and after *Aiguebelle* you rejoin the Isère valley. Turn right and soon reach *Albertville*. From there return by the outward route. 360 km. for round trip (320 km. by the Little St. Bernard Pass).

Champex lake

One of the most popular day trips from Chamonix, of moderate distance. The drive is almost identical to the first part of the Mt. Blanc Road Tour.

Leave Chamonix by the main road up the valley to *Argentière* and cross the *Col des Montets* to *Vallorcine*. The Mt. Blanc range is always to the rear and now recedes from view. Swiss frontier at *Le Châtelard*. The road crosses the river, goes through the Roche Percée tunnel and contours the Tête Noire in a semi-circle to the east, above the Eau Noire gorge and with Finhaut on the opposite side. Reach the gay Swiss resort of *Trient*, after which the road returns in a zigzag above the village and climbs steeply to the *Col de la Forclaz* (1527 m.). Cableway. Grand view of the Aig. du Tour at the north extremity of Mt. Blanc range. On the other side of the pass you descend in wide zigzags through vineyards and meadows to join the Great St. Bernard road on the outskirts of *Martigny*. This is the Drance valley. Turn right, away from Martigny, and drive to *Sembrancher* and *Orsières*. Turn right at Orsières, off the Great St. Bernard road, into the *Val Ferret* and reach the first village, *Som la Praz*, in 2 km. Turn right and climb an excellent little road in many zigzags to the *Lac de Champex* and the fashionable resort in pretty surroundings on the east shore. 60 km. from Chamonix. Splendid view to south-east of the Grand Combin (4314 m.), monarch of the Western Pennine Alps. Chairlift to La Breya; magnificent panorama. Return by same route.

On the last stage to Champex a more interesting and exciting variation, and a short cut avoiding the big corner formed in the Drance valley at Sembrancher, is to follow a narrow, steep and twisting road above the Durnand gorges. After reaching the Great St. Bernard road (Drance valley) near Martigny, about 3 km. further turn right at the village of *Les Valettes*. This road is exceedingly picturesque, with startling views into wild glens to the west. You reach the hamlets of Champex d'en Bas and d'en Haut before crossing a broad saddle to the lake. Recommended for outward journey. About 8 km. shorter.

Mt. Blanc Road Tour

The classic motoring itinerary of the region. It was devised by tour operators after the 1914–18 War, when the major road passes became practicable for charabancs. In those days the Tour took two or three days, according to the sightseeing diversions offered. It is now easily accomplished in a day with adequate halts.

The Mt. Blanc Tour derives from a much closer circuit on foot round the Mt. Blanc range (see Section five). The road connections so linked to form the Road Tour amount to a fairly roundabout itinerary. All the same, the scenery is outstanding, though apart from classic views of Mt. Blanc in the Chamonix valley, and the singularly mighty mass rising at the head of the Aosta valley, not a lot is seen of the remainder of the range unless detours are made from Courmayeur up the Val Veni and Italian Val Ferret, which together represent the Italian equivalent to the Chamonix valley. This defect is compensated by quite remarkable views of great peaks in the Pennine Alps and Gran Paradiso National Park.

The Mt. Blanc tunnel affords a short cut to the original itinerary. The original route is described and the short cut is appended as a variation. The route is obviously reversible, but in the direction described more of the best scenery is ahead of you instead of behind.

Large sections of the Tour overlap with sections of other day trips described in the previous pages. To avoid repeated cross-references these sections are described in full again.

Leave Chamonix by the main road up the valley to *Argentière* and cross the *Col des Montets* to *Vallorcine*. The Mt. Blanc range is always to the rear and now recedes from view. Swiss frontier at *Le Châtelard*. The road crosses the river, goes through the Roche Percée tunnel and contours the Tête Noire in a semi-circle to the east, above the Eau Noire gorge and with Finhaut on the opposite side. Reach the gay Swiss resort of *Trient*, after which the road returns in a zigzag above the village and climbs steeply to the *Col de la Forclaz* (1527 m.). Cableway. Grand view of the Aig. du Tour at the northern extremity of Mt. Blanc range. On the other side of the pass you descend in wide zigzags through vineyards and meadows to join the Great St. Bernard road on the outskirts of *Martigny*. Glimpses of the Bernese Alps across the great opening of the Rhône valley beyond Martigny in which the Balmhorn (3709 m.) and Bietschhorn (3934 m.) can be identified.

You have now reached the Drance valley. Turn right, away from Martigny, and drive to *Sembrancher* and *Orsières*. From Orsières the main road to the Great St. Bernard pass climbs leftwards in a picturesque forested valley with open meadowlands. In the past few years most of this road has been rebuilt at a somewhat higher level to avoid the villages of Liddes and Bourg St. Pierre as you approach the pass. The gradient is moderate, sharp bends are few and far between until the final stage below the top is reached, and the surface is of autobahn standard. Soon after Orsières you catch a sight of *Mt. Velan* (3734 m.). The valley is extensively cultivated and beyond *Liddes* and *Bourg St. Pierre* (famous mountaineering centre for the Grand Combin district) the road is covered by an impressive gallery, almost like a tunnel, built along the mountain-side to protect it in winter from snow and avalanches. This covered way leads to the tunnel that pierces the Great St. Bernard pass. The *tunnel* (toll charge) is much shorter than driving over the top, but this avoids one of the best moments on the tour. Its main purpose is for winter motoring when the road over the pass is always closed by snow. At the entrance to the tunnel, called *Super St. Bernard*, restaurant, shop and cableway to 2800 m. (superb views of Mt. Velan and Mt. Blanc range).

The final section enters a wild narrow valley; sharp bends lead into the gloomy Combe des Morts (snow patches) before the conglomeration of buildings, old and new, are reached at the *summit* (2469 m.). The famous *hospice* is open to the public, with dogs in attendance; hotel and restaurants, shops, souvenir stalls, and lake. Cableway to Chenalette (Swiss enterprise). At the far end of the lake the road resembles a thoroughfare in an oriental market and is somewhat out of keeping with the surroundings. Swiss and Italian customs.

The site of the Roman temple of Jupiter Penninus, from which the pass took its medieval name of Mons Jovis or Montjoux, is still marked by steps cut into the rock, but no part of the building remains. Many inscriptions and other objects of interest have been found here and are preserved in the museum in the hospice. The original hospice was at Bourg St. Pierre, but possibly even before the Saracen raids in the 10th century had been transferred to the summit of the pass. It was certainly refounded there in 962 by St. Bernard of Menthon (hence the present name), and since the 12th century remained in charge of a community of Austin Canons Regular. In the 18th and 19th centuries the majority of passers-by were fed and sheltered gratuitously. No demand was made from the traveller for pleasure, who was always entertained in a superior way. Towards the end of this period it became generally understood that those who could afford it should give at least as much as they would pay in an ordinary hotel. The army of Napoleon Bonaparte crossed the pass in 1800.

The English traveller Brockedon reports (1838): 'Travellers are passing every day during the winter, notwithstanding the perils of such a pass at such times. These persons, when they arrive at a certain house not far from the summit, are desired to wait till the following morning, when a servant and a dog descend from the top to this kind of refuge, and take up all the persons assembled, the servant being conducted by the dog, who, it appears, never misses the way, but, entirely hidden, except his tail, in the snow, directs the march of the whole cavalcade. The stories about the monks going out searching for lost travellers, and the dogs carrying wine, are false in toto.'

The road descending the Italian side of the pass is less good than the Swiss. It is both narrower and rougher. It winds at first and views to the south open out gradually. You pass quite close to the foot of small but striking rock peaks, with large blocks strewn about the slopes and snow patches lying in gullies. You can soon see into the cultivated valley below. The road passes under the cantilevered highway of the new spur coming from the *Italian entrance to the tunnel*, which makes a great loop to the west. The old road descends to *St. Rhémy* and *Étroubles*. The notorious heat of the Aosta valley below is now evident, on the far side of which you see the high mass of *Mt. Emilius* (3559 m.). At the hamlet of *Gignod* there is a superb view to the left (east) up the entire length of the remote *Valpelline*, with the *Dents d'Hérens* (4171 m.) at its head. A view of the Matterhorn is only just missed. Due north (behind) there are fine views of the *Grand Combin* massif (4314 m.). In a few more kilometres you reach the north ring road round *Aosta* (traffic lights). Either continue ahead into the town for a halt here, or turn right and follow the road up the Aosta valley in the Courmayeur direction.

The main road in the Aosta valley is fast and busy. On the left (south) you have splendid views of sharp peaks on the edge of the Gran Paradiso National Park, notably of *La Grivola* (3969 m.). The valley has vineyards and a number of ancient castles on its lower slopes. The astonishing snowy mass of *Mt. Blanc* fills the skyline ahead. At the top of the valley keep a sharp lookout for a slip road on the left to *Pré St. Didier*. Straight ahead is the new road leading past *Courmayeur* to the *Mt. Blanc tunnel* and *Chamonix*.

Follow the old main road through Pré St. Didier and climb steadily to *La Thuile* and the *Little St. Bernard pass* (2188 m.). Near the top, behind you, is a magnificent scene including the Mt. Blanc range, the Grand Combin and Mt. Velan. Ahead, a superb view of *Mt. Pourri* (3779 m.) and other snowy peaks in the Tarentaise massif of the Graian Alps. St. Bernard of Menthon also founded the hospice on this pass as well as the better known one the Great St. Bernard. Druidical circle, inn, restaurant, lake. Italian and French customs. The pass is of considerable historical importance and some researchers believe that it was the pass crossed by *Hannibal's army* and elephants during his invasion of Italy (not supported by more recent investigations).

On the other side descend easily with zigzags to finish into the Isère valley at *Séez village*. Bear right and continue down to *Bourg St. Maurice*. Follow the main road in the Isère valley to *Moûtiers-Salins* and *Albertville*, then turn right along R.N. 212 to *Ugine*. Continue through the Arly gorges to *Flumet*, *Megève* and keep right on R.N. 509 to reach *St. Gervais* and *Le Fayet*. Return up the Chamonix valley. About 310 km. for round trip.

It is so much shorter to avoid the Little St. Bernard pass by taking the new motor road through the Mt. Blanc tunnel that most people will prefer this short cut back to Chamonix. On the motorway at the top of the Aosta valley keep right at the turning for **Pré St.** Didier and continue to the tunnel. About 180 km. for round trip.

10 Excursions by coach or regular bus services

Day trips from Chamonix are exactly the same itineraries for those described by car. A number of excursions can be made to places further afield. Tickets can be bought to include a mid-day meal. According to itinerary one or more stops are made for sightseeing.

The table below summarises the services available. Address all inquiries to Catella, Ave. de la Gare; or tourist office.

To	Normal departure Chamonix	Normal return Chamonix	Tours per week
Gorges de la Diose*	14.00	18.00	7
Assy chapel and Lac Vert*	14.00	18.00	7
Courmayeur andAosta*	13.00	18.00	7
Cols des Aravis and de la Colombière	13.00	20.00	1
Sixt and Fer à Cheval	13.00	20.00	1
Geneva and Lake*	07.30	20.00	7
Lake Geneva Tour	06.00	20.00	3
Annecy and Lake*	07.30	20.00	7
Col de l'Iseran circuit	06.00	20.00	1
Champex lake	09.00	18.00	1
Mont Blanc Road Tour	06.00	20.00	6
Great St. Bernard pass	07.00	19.00	7
Interlaken	06.00	20.30	3
Evian	07.30	20.00	2
Milan	07.30	20.00	2

An asterisk indicates that the route is also served by a regular public bus service. However, all routes can be done by public transport with one or more changes.

Section five

Tour of Mont Blanc

This is a walking route, with many possible variations, round the Mt. Blanc range. It is probably the most famous and finest walk of its kind in the Alps. Joint agreement between French, Italian and Swiss authorities ensures that the trails used to complete the walk are kept in good order, and that waymarks and signposts are maintained. There is an official version of the Tour, with variations, but many other detours, shorter and longer, can be made according to weather, ambition or inclination. The official route does not touch the snowline and glaciers are avoided. This route is the one adopted by the Chamonix Guides' Bureau for conducted parties which leave weekly in the summer. Six to eight days are usually allowed for completing the circuit, although anything between five and nine days could be occupied, depending on the pace of a party and the route chosen.

In France today, walking routes of regional and international interest are defined, classified and co-ordinated by a government-sponsored body called the Comité National des Sentiers de Grande Randonnée (C.N.S.G.R.). About 10 key trails and nearly 100 regional walks have been classified and described since this body began its work in 1947. The trails are designated numerically, viz. G.R. 1, G.R. 2, G.R. 3, etc., and the longest of them is G.R. 5 which extends for 1200 km. from Luxemburg to the Mediterranean. This trail traverses the whole of the French Alps from north to south and approaches the Chamonix region by using part of the Tour of Mt. Blanc. All G.R. routes and associated regional walks are waymarked with red and white paint flashes. G.R. 5 approaches the Mt. Blanc region via Sixt and continues southwards by the Col d'Anterne, Col du Brévent, Les Houches, Col de Vose, Les Contamines and the Col du Bonhomme. In the Mt. Blanc district paths are the responsibility of the council of the commune and the mountain rescue societies of Chamonix and St. Gervais.

Being shared between France, Italy and Switzerland, the Tour of Mt. Blanc has no G.R. number of its own but it is promoted by all three countries as one of their finest mountain rambles. It has the advantage that you are rarely far from a habitation in case of prolonged bad weather. With a little common sense the walk is absolutely safe, and those who would not call themselves strong walkers can adjust daily stages to suit themselves. The scenery throughout is magnificent; the range is seen from all quarters at close quarters, and from points where no motorised visitor could drive a car. It goes without saying that proper clothing and stout boots which must be comfortable are essential; so is a 50,000 scale map and a compass. Above all it is vital for comfort to make the tour with a rucksack of minimum weight; discard everything that is not absolutely necessary. Those who wish to avoid the expense of staying overnight in mountain huts and inns at the end of daily stages might choose to camp, but only fit and hardy walkers will be able to cope with the extra gear required. Cableways and public transport can be used on some stages; this is usual for conducted parties starting from Chamonix which set out to accomplish the walk in six days.

A full description of the Tour of Mt. Blanc would occupy a separate guidebook (one is in preparation). A brief description of the route, ignoring some popular variations, is given below in eight daily stages.

1st day *Chamonix—Les Houches—Nant Borrant. 7–8 h.*
Bus from Chamonix to Les Houches, then by the Bellevue cableway to the Col de Vose. Trail descends via the chalets and hamlet of Les Crozats to Le Champel and La Villette in the Val Montjoie. Walk or take a bus up this valley to roadhead at Notre-Dame de la Gorge. Continue up the main valley to the small hotel at Nant Borrant, or to the chalet-inn at the Balme, 1 h. further.

2nd day *Nant Borrant (Balme)—*
Col du Bonhomme—Chapieux. 7 h.
The main footpath is followed in the valley bed over two steps to the Col du Bonhomme (2329 m.), then you traverse the mountain-side before descending to the Raja chalets and the hamlet of Les Chapieux. Inn.

3rd day *Les Chapieux—Col de la Seigne—Elisabetta hut. 5 h.*
You walk north-east up a small road in the straight Glaciers valley to the chalets of Ville des Glaciers. Then cross to the other side of the stream and climb a good path to the Col de la Seigne (2513 m.), under the Aigs. des Glaciers. Italian frontier. An easy

descent into the Val Veni leads to the Elisabetta hut
(C.A.I.). Restaurant and dormitory accommodation.

4th day *Elisabetta hut–Entrèves/Courmayeur. 4 h.*
The easiest stage of the walk. Below the hut a short
zigzag track joins a small unmade road descending the
bed of the Val Veni, almost flat, along the edge of old
moraines and under the Miage moraine crest to
forest below. At the village of Visaille there is a bus
service to Courmayeur. Because the views of the
Italian side of the Mt. Blanc range are superb, it is
more rewarding to walk down. After Visaille the road
can be avoided by a good path at a higher level,
rejoining the road again at Notre-Dame de Guérison.
The road bends right to Courmayeur, which lies
below the junction of the Val Veni and Val Ferret,
where Entrèves is situated. Courmayeur can be
avoided by descending left to the river below the
Brenva glacier ; there cross the motorway coming
from the tunnel entrance nearby and reach Entrèves
on the other side. Hotels and pensions.

5th day *Courmayeur/Entrèves–Arnuva chalet. 4 h.*
This is also an easy stage, up the Val Ferret, in which
there is a small road. Beyond Lavanchey, and after
the zigzag bends in the road, a path on the right
should be taken instead of the road for the last bit
to the Arnuva inn. A little further up the valley the
Elena hut (C.A.I.) is being repaired and may be open
soon.

6th day *Arnuva chalet–Grand Col Ferret–*
Champex lake. 9 h.
One of the longest day-stages, and an early start is
advised. A good trail up the last bit of the Val Ferret
leads to a junction at the Pré de Bar chalets. Turn
sharp right for the Grand Col Ferret (2537 m.), which
is reached by a steep but comfortable path. Swiss
frontier. Descend gradually into the head of the Swiss
Val Ferret, where a road is found at the bottom. This
goes down to La Fouly village, the mountaineering
centre of the district. Post bus service down to
Orsières at the bottom of the valley. From La Fouly
the correct walking route avoids the road by a pleasant
path on the opposite (west) side of the river. Reach
Praz de Fort, then Issert, where the trail mounts

forested slopes to Champex. All kinds of accommodation, etc.

7th day *Champex lake–Col de la Forclaz–Trient–Col de Balme–Le Tour. 12 h.*

The longest stage of the Tour. Some walkers have been known to give up at Trient and take a bus back to Chamonix. This misses one of the best viewpoints on the walk. The chairlift can be used at the Col de Balme to eliminate walking down to Le Tour.

Follow the small road out of Champex to the northwest, then take a trail on the left. This joins the road again momentarily, before finally bearing away to the west, across the Plan de l'Au forest. The trail traverses in and out of grassy combes and pastures in a line to the west to reach the Col de la Forclaz. Main road and cableway. Descend southwards below the road, cross it after the last bend and walk away from Trient by a steep path in woods above the Nant Noir stream, coming down from the Col de Balme (2191 m.). So reach this col and the French frontier. From here descend the large easy path to Le Tour, or use cableway to your left (south).

8th day *Le Tour–Plan des Aigs. Rouges–Chamonix. 5–8 h.*

The last stage traverses the great terrace under the Aigs. Rouges above the Chamonix valley. Strictly speaking you should continue over the Brévent to Les Houches, then return up the valley. However, few if any parties go to these lengths. It is more usual to descend from La Flégère, on foot or by cableway. Those who feel up to it can continue to the Brévent and descend from there.

From Le Tour the road is followed to Montroc station. Near the entrance to the railway tunnel a path to the left leads to the main road at Trélechamp hamlet, from where the trail climbs south towards the Aiguillette chairlift. You continue by paths rising to the Chéserys chalets, and along to La Flégère and the Brévent. This stage is covered in some detail in various walks described in Sections One and Three.

Section six

Mountaineering at Chamonix

In the 19th century nearly all the reliable information at the time on mountaineering in the Mt. Blanc range was available in English. For the next 50 years nothing in the way of guidebooks appeared for the English-speaking climber, till the 1950s. In 1967 the Alpine Club revived its series of pocket guides, and the Mt. Blanc range in two volumes was the first area to be covered.

Climbing guidebooks are traditionally clinical and matter-of-fact in their treatment of mountains, and route descriptions tend to be highly technical and consequently brief. In an age when climbing has become more of a sport with competitive motives than a pastime, all material that can be classified as pertaining to the spiritual aspects of mountaineering becomes superfluous. For example these guidebooks rarely examine the surrounding scenery and the effect this might have in choosing particular climbs. The other side of the picture is that climbs which are technically interesting can be found in scenically dull places.

The main reason for including a section on mountaineering in this all-purpose guidebook is to indicate the extent of professional services available to beginners, and to itemise a few of the hundreds of first-class routes in the region that are of exceptional interest to the learner. In not a few cases enthusiasm is uncertain till the climber has done sufficient climbing to decide whether or not he likes it. Many good climbs have laborious or difficult approaches before the pleasure begins. The novice can be misled by failing to understand the cryptic language used in technical descriptions, which tend to dismiss tedious approaches in a few words. Indeed such guidebooks are not designed for use by novices, and in the writing assume a seasoned knowledge of alpinism. But they are used by all-comers.

Today, expense is a real consideration in mountaineering. Guideless climbing predominates among all nationalities with its attendant risks for inexperienced persons. Perhaps the most important factor to emerge will be the weather; in a matter of minutes a simple climb can be transformed into a death-trap. Apart from serving what was once called an apprenticeship with competent friends, usually through a club, the only means of acquiring the knowledge necessary for safe mountaineering is to join a course organised by professional instructors or guides.

Hiring a guide to undertake particular climbs is still the most expensive way of learning to climb. On the other hand, if you can afford it and have the physical constitution, it is undoubtedly the quickest way, and weather permitting you will cover a lot of ground in a short time. In practice guides are often engaged for particular climbs that may be just outside the reach of a client in terms of guideless leadership and experience, and this can be a short cut to improving confidence and experience. If you are not safe with a guide, you are safe with nobody.

1 Climbing

If employing a guide today is a luxury, the situation is plainly economic. The demand for guiding services has diminished in proportion with the numbers of visitors who come to Chamonix solely for mountaineering. Professionals are less sure of obtaining continuous employment. Moreover the summer season is barely four months long and guides who determine to make a career of this profession continue as skiing instructors in winter, and guide overland ski-touring parties in spring. Regulations governing the enrolment and training of guides are very strict and serving an apprenticeship is long and hard. Insurances and guarantees of security provided by the State add up to a sophisticated, increasingly complex and costly service, and charges are pitched accordingly. A well-known discrepancy in the scale of charges is that a big or important mountain of little technical difficulty often carries a higher fee than a smaller and perhaps technically more difficult climb. Evidence of this can be seen in the table below. So much emphasis is put on 'collectives' by the Guides' Bureau at Chamonix that, while serving to attract more business because of lower charges, these schemes are bound to provide the most practical way of starting to climb. An indication of fees for standard routes is as follows:

Mountain/climb	Height (m.)	Grade*	Type of climb	Fee £ sterling
Mont Blanc, ordinary route	4807	I	snow	30
Aig. de l'M., NNE ridge	2844	IV	rock	10
Grépon, ordinary traverse	3482	IV	rock	20
Grépon, Mer de Glace face	3482	IV/V	rock	30
Grépon, Charmoz traverse	3482	IV	rock	25
Midi–Plan traverse	3842	II	mixed	20
Tour Ronde, ordinary route	3792	II	snow	13
Petit Dru, ordinary route	3733	IV	rock	30
Drus, traverse	3754	IV	rock	37
Les Courtes, ordinary route	3856	II	mixed	24
Moine, ordinary route	3412	II	rock	16
Chardonnet, ordinary traverse	3824	II/III	snow	21
Aig. du Tour	3544	I	snow	14
Peigne, ordinary route	3192	III	rock	14

*Grades of difficulty for rock climbs are indicated by roman numerals I to VI (VI being the hardest). Snow and ice climbs are classified by another system but for simple comparison the rock grades are used.

Several of these climbs can be done for rather more than one-third of the fee in collective courses.

It is much cheaper to join a professionally supervised collective or course where fees are lower because costs are shared by a number of persons. Several types of group activity are organised by the Guides' Bureau. The main ones are:

1 Climbing school with progressive instruction on hourly, daily, or weekly basis.
2 Walking excursions over set itineraries; one, two, three or more consecutive days.
3 Tour of Mt. Blanc; parties leave once a week.
4 Summer ski school and instruction; three locations.

Enrolment takes place at the bureaux in Chamonix or Argentière. Locations used by the climbing school are as follows:

	Location	Type of instruction
Gaillands rockface	off main road, opposite Les Pèlerins	rock-climbing techniques
Mer de Glace	Montenvers	ice-climbing techniques
Brévent	adjacent summit rocks	rope techniques
Petite Aig. Verte	top station, Grands Montets cableway	snow-climbing techniques

	Location	*Type of instruction*
Aig. de l'M.	Montenvers	practical rock climbing
Petits Charmoz	Montenvers	general rock climbing
Aig. du Midi	top station, Midi cableway	techniques for mixed terrain
Aig. du Tour	Albert I hut	glacier travel

Various huts are also used for general mountaineering.

The climbing school is operated on a period course fee and on a ticket basis. You hand in so many tickets according to what you feel like trying or taking part in. The price of tickets reduces slightly if more are bought at the same time. Approximate costs are as follows:

1 ticket   16s.
3 tickets   £2. 5s.
6 tickets   £4. 5s.

An illustration of the value of tickets can be given as follows:

1 rock climbing or ice climbing lesson of 3 hours:
2 tickets

Whole day of instruction in any technique, or mixed techniques, according to location:
6 tickets

36 hours of instruction, inclusive of spending night in mountain hut:
6–10 tickets

For comparative purposes, private tuition with your own guide costs about £2. 10s. per hour, or £7. 10s. for 3 hours (2 tickets = £1. 12s.).

If your group is small and its members look promising, the guide will have no hesitation taking the party up a comparatively good climb on an important peak, if the climb can be done in a day, up and down from Chamonix. Three persons are usually the minimum number that will be considered for this, and one of the party may be required to lead a second rope on easier parts of the climb. Encouragement to lead is fundamental in all mountaineering instruction.

Ordinarily, if you hire a guide as a private client to visit mountain huts—the majority of which in the Mt. Blanc range are not really suitable as walks for unaccompanied inexperienced persons—the fee can be anything up to 100 francs, or about £8. Group visits to huts have proved so popular, often in conjunction with making a climb from the hut, that every day of the week there is an organised party setting out on different excursions. Some of these include:

Aig. de l'M. £4
Requin hut and Vallée Blanche £5
Grands Mulets hut £5
Leschaux hut £2
Couvercle hut and the Jardin £2. 5s.
Aig. du Tour (Albert I hut) £5
Three classic cols of Tour glacier basin £6

The Tour of Mt. Blanc is a weekly feature in the programme of walking excursions. Charges are inclusive of transport, lodging, meals and guiding services:

Complete tour of six days £26

If you leave the party before returning to Chamonix, part fees are: Four days £18   Two days £10.

12 Skiing

Ski instruction takes place at three locations during summer, and generally only in the mornings, between 07.00 and 13.00 h. Normally the snow is not good enough in the afternoon and on a fine day the heat can be uncomfortable. Fees vary according to location and the number of persons taking part. Fees are always inclusive of using cableways to the ski-fields and skilifts once you get there. The locations are:

Grands Montets	2 skilifts rising through 250 m.
Index snowfields	1 skilift rising through 90 m.
Col du Géant	3 skilifts, with maximum rise of 200 m.

Ski tours in the springtime and early summer are much more ambitious undertakings and a degree of experience is a necessary qualification for joining these courses. There are a number of other requirements, including membership of a continental Alpine club. The finest tour organised regularly by the Chamonix guides is the High Level Route to Zermatt, which is fitted into a programme lasting seven days. The all-inclusive cost is about £50.

13 Recommended routes

In this section reference is made to volume and route numbers in *Selected Climbs in the Mont Blanc Range*, as indicated in the list of abbreviations in the front of the guidebook. These recommendations are intended as a guide to all-comers, but it is emphasised that genuine mountaineering ability is needed for making any of these climbs in safety—and all that goes with it—especially if you are a guideless party. The selection is fairly short and an attempt has been made to include only the best climbs of their class, for interest, scenery, fine situations, and lack of monotony during the approach. Grades of difficulty are indicated by numeral I–IV.

Climb and grade	Remarks	Ref.
Mont Tondu 3196 m. Main ridge traverse I *from Trélatête inn*	Mixed climbing. Care needed to find correct way up to ridge. Fine knobbly crest to summit. Superb views	**I, 29**
Dômes de Miage 3673 m. Main ridge traverse I/II *from Trélatête inn*	Best introduction to snow-ridge climbing in region. Long scenic approach on glacier with hidden crevasses	**I, 40**
Mt. Blanc 4807 m. Ordinary routes I *from Grands Mulets/Tête Rousse/Goûter huts*	Gradual snow climbing, with narrow ridge to finish. Outstanding glacier scenery. Tiring unless you are fit	**I, 45, 46**
Bionnassay traverse III *from Durier hut*	Delicate corniced snow ridge in fine position. Remote and serious	**I, 41, 42, 45**
Midi–Plan 3842 m. Traverse III *from Midi cableway/Requin hut*	Mixed climbing on exposed ridge over main valley	**I, 118**
Requin 3422 m. Normal route III *from Requin hut*	Rock climb on perfect granite with short approach on steep mixed terrain	**I, 131**
Pèlerins 3318 m. Normal route II *from Plan cableway*	Pleasant, old fashioned climbing with mock-serious air. Icy late in season	**I, 140**
Peigne 3192 m. Normal route III *from Plan cableway*	Good rock climb, serious of its kind, route finding tricky in Peigne couloir, stonefall danger	**I, 144**

Climb and grade	Remarks	Ref.
Blaitière 3522 m. Spencer couloir or Corde **III** *from Montenvers/Plan*	Enchanting climb on snow and rocks. For safety, must be in good condition. Best views of Chamonix Aiguilles	**I, 160** **161**
Grépon 3482 m. Traverse **IV** *from Montenvers/Plan*	Best-known rock climb at Chamonix. Beautiful pitches on firm rock. Mixed rock/glacier approach, steep, serious, ice-fall danger	**I, 168**
Grands Charmoz 3444 m. Traverse **IV** *from Montenvers/Plan*	Justly famous rock climb, only slightly less variety than Grépon; often combined	**I, 172**
Petits Charmoz 2867 m. Traverse **II** *from Montenvers/Plan*	Excellent training climb for novices, short rock pitches, no mystery about route finding	**I, 175**
Aig. de l'M. 2844 m. Normal route **II** *from Montenvers/Plan*	Very popular little peak nearest to Chamonix. Last 30 m. variable and confusing	**I, 176**
North-north-east ridge **IV** *from Montenvers*	Technical rock climb with hard smooth pitches	**I, 176**
Aig. du Géant 4013 m. Normal route **III** *Géant/Torino hut*	Great rock finger hardly spoiled by fixed ropes. Glacier and mixed approach, short but needing care. Superb views	**II, 25**
Rochefort ridge 4001 m. Traverse **III** *Géant/Torino hut*	Same approach as Géant, corniced snow crest, technically interesting	**II, 28**
Ravanel/Mummery 3700 m. Traverse **IV** *from Couvercle hut*	Classic rock climbs, very exposed and slightly muscular. Interesting approach on mixed terrain	**II, 68** **to** **70**
Les Courtes 3856 m. Traverse **II/III** *from Couvercle hut*	Fine mixed climb, requires good conditions, sensational views. Crevassed glacier	**II, 74**
Aig. Verte 4122 m. Whymper couloir/Moine ridge **III** *from Couvercle hut*	Serious mixed climbs on a difficult mountain with objective dangers. Requires good technique and fore-sight for safety and enjoyment	**II, 82,** **84**

Climb and grade	Remarks	Ref.
La Nonne 3340 m. Traverse **II** *from Couvercle hut*	Short rock climb of quality and interest, close to hut	**II, 94**
Moine 3412 m. Various **II/IV** *from Couvercle hut*	Classic rock climb and viewpoint, short approach. Bergschrund below rockface can be awkward	**II, 95, 96**
Grand Dru 3754 m. Ordinary route **III** *from Charpoua hut*	Magnificent rock climb with awkward glacier approach. Technical descent, wild scenery	**II, 100**
Petit Dru 3733 m. Ordinary route **IV** *from Charpoua hut*	Superb, strenuous rock climb, continuously difficult in top half. Technical descent needing care	**II, 101**
Drus traverse **IV** *from Charpoua hut*	The two previous routes combined, unrivalled rock climbing interest and situations. Long and hard for its standard	**II, 102**
Aig. d'Argentière 3900 m. Milieu glacier route **II** *from Argentière hut*	One of the best snow climbs of its class in region, very popular, short, with outstanding view of Swiss portion of range. Icy late in season	**II, 114**
Chardonnet 3824 m. Traverse **II/III** *from Albert I hut*	Fine exposed snow ridge with short rock pitches, airy and delicate. Crevassed glacier on descent	**II, 120**
Purtscheller 3478 m. South ridge **III/IV** *from Albert I hut*	Popular rock climb with several variations. Flat glacier approach	**II, 128**
Aig. du Tour 3544 m. Various **I/II** *from Albert I hut*	Perennial snow climb with easy rocks, classic view along north side of Mt. Blanc range	**II, 130 to 133**

Summit of the Requin. All the main peaks of the Chamonix Aiguilles finish with dramatic pinnacles. This one is climbed more or less up the right-hand edge. For descending, you use a doubled rope to swing down the deep chimney in the middle

Climbing on the Chamonix Aiguilles. To save time, skilful climbers are able to move together confidently on rock with good holds. A party moves one at a time when particularly difficult or steep sections of rock occur

Trainee mountain guides receiving instruction in Chamonix, using a relief model of the Mt. Blanc range

Descending beside an icefall. Note how the rope is kept off the surface of the glacier so that there is no slack or play in it. This minimises the jerk in the event of a member of the party falling into a crevasse

Appendix I

Principal peaks of the Mont Blanc range

Mountains that can only be seen properly from the Italian (Courmayeur) side of the range are marked thus in brackets. Brévent, etc. = Brévent, Planpraz, La Flégère. Listed in order from south-west to north-east.

Mountain	Height (m.)	Best viewpoint(s)
Mt. Tondu	3196	—
Aig. des Glaciers	3816	(Courmayeur)
Aigs. de Trélatête	3930	(Courmayeur)
Dômes de Miage	3670	Vose/Prarion
Aig. de Bionnassay	4051	Vose/Tête Rousse
Mt. Blanc	4807	Brévent, etc./Midi–Géant télé.
Dôme du Goûter	4304	Brévent, etc./Tête Rousse
Aig. du Goûter	3863	Brévent, etc./Tête Rousse
Mt. Maudit	4465	Brévent, etc./Midi–Géant télé.
Mt. Blanc du Tacul	4248	Brévent, etc./Midi–Géant télé.
Aigs. du Diable	4114	Midi–Géant télé.
Aig. Blanche	4108	Géant–Torino télé.
Aig. Noire	3773	Géant–Torino télé.
Tour Ronde	3792	Midi–Géant télé.
Aig. du Géant	4013	Midi–Géant télé.
Grandes Jorasses	4208	Montenvers/Midi–Géant télé.
Chamonix Aiguilles Midi, Plan, Requin, Fou, Crocodile, Grépon, Charmoz, etc.	3500– 3800	Brévent, etc./Plan de l'Aiguille/Montenvers/Grands Montets
Aig. de Triolet	3870	Couvercle/Jardin
Les Courtes	3856	Couvercle/Jardin
Les Droites	4000	Couvercle/Jardin
Aig. Verte	4122	Brévent, etc./Montenvers/ Grands Montets/Aiguillette
Aig. du Dru (Drus)	3754	Brévent, etc./Montenvers
Mt. Dolent	3823	Grands Montets
Tour Noir	3837	Grands Montets
Aig. d'Argentière	3900	Grands Montets
Aig. du Chardonnet	3824	Grands Montets/Albert I hut
Aig. du Tour	3544	Albert I hut

Appendix II

Mountain huts (Refuges)
in the Chamonix district

This is not a complete list for the whole range; huts reached directly from Chamonix and providing a restaurant service are included, with a note of two others of interest to climbers. These huts have accommodation for 50 or more persons, some more than 100. The traditional term of 'hut' is still used, although these buildings are much larger than the name implies.

Hut	Altitude (m.)	Location	Hours on foot
Tête Rousse	3167	foot of Aig. du Goûter	3 h. from tramway
Goûter	3817	top of Goûter peak	3 h. from Tête Rousse
Grands Mulets	3051	above junction of Bossons/ Taconnaz glaciers	3 h. from Plan
Envers des Aigs.	2523	foot of Aigs., Mer de Glace side	3 h. from Montenvers
Requin	2516	beside Géant icefall	$3\frac{1}{2}$ h. from Montenvers
Torino/ Géant	3322	hotel on col, hut below next to cableway	3 h. from Requin hut, or by cableway
Couvercle	2687	right bank Talèfre glacier, below Moine	4 h. from Montenvers
Argentière	2771	right bank of glacier, below peak of same name	$5\frac{1}{2}$ h. from Argentière village, 2 h. from Grands Montets
Albert I	2702	right bank Tour glacier	$3\frac{1}{2}$ h. from Le Tour, 2 h. from Balme cableway

With plain sleeping quarters and no warden as a rule (self-cooking):

Charpoua	2841	below glacier on south side of Drus	3 h. from Montenvers
Leschaux	2431	right bank of Leschaux glacier	$3\frac{1}{2}$ h. from Montenvers

Appendix III

**Train and bus fare stages
in Chamonix valley**

A specimen timetable is chosen at random to indicate journey times. Places in italics are wayside halts which can only be used by advising the conductor.

Train		*Bus*	
Le Fayet	08.45		
Chedde	08.48		
Servoz	08.56		
Vaudagne	08.59		
Ste.-Marie	09.01		
Les Houches	09.05	Les Houches	08.35
Taconnaz	09.09	Le Mont	08.50
Les Bossons	09.12		
Les Pèlerins	09.14		
Les Moussoux	09.16		
Chamonix arr.	09.20	**Chamonix**	09.00
dep.	09.30		
Les Praz	09.33	Les Praz/Flégère	09.05
Les Tines	09.36	Chosalets/Lognan	09.15
La Joux	09.40		
Argentière	09.44	Argentière	09.20
Montroc	09.51	Le Tour	09.30
Le Buet	09.57		
Vallorcine arr.	10.02		
dep.	10.10		
Martigny arr.	11.13		

There are about 15 trains a day, up and down the valley, and about the same number of buses.

Appendix IV

Postal rates

Inland (France)   *Francs*
Letters (up to 20 grams) 1st class   0.40
                                     2nd class   0.30
Postcards   0.30

Abroad
Letters (up to 20 grams)   0.70
                  per 20 grams intervals   0.40
Postcards, 5 words of greeting   0.25
Postcards, otherwise   0.40

except:
Germany, Belgium, Canada,
Luxemburg, Italy:
Letters   0.30
All Postcards   0.25

Appendix V

Conversion tables, measurement

Centimetres–inches

Cm.	In. or cm.	In.
2·540	1	0·394
5·080	2	0·787
7·620	3	1·181
10·160	4	1·575
12·700	5	1·969
15·240	6	2·362
17·780	7	2·756
20·320	8	3·150
22·860	9	3·543
25·400	10	3·937
50·800	20	7·874
63·500	25	9·843
127·00	50	19·685
254·000	100	39·370

Metres–feet

Metres	Feet or metres	Feet
0·305	1	3·281
0·610	2	6·562
0·914	3	9·842
1·219	4	13·123
1·524	5	16·404
1·829	6	19·685
2·134	7	22·966
2·438	8	26·247
2·743	9	29·528
3·048	10	32·808
6·096	20	65·616
7·620	25	82·022
15·240	50	164·043
30·480	100	328·086

Metres–yards

Metres	Yards or metres	Yards
0·914	1	1·094
1·829	2	2·187
2·743	3	3·281
3·658	4	4·374
4·572	5	5·468
5·486	6	6·562
6·401	7	7·655
7·315	8	8·749
8·230	9	9·843
9·144	10	10·936
18·288	20	21·872
22·860	25	27·340
45·720	50	54·681
91·439	100	109·361

Kilometres–miles

Km.	Miles or km.	Miles
1·609	1	0·621
3·218	2	1·242
4·827	3	1·864
6·437	4	2·485
8·046	5	3·107
9·655	6	3·728
11·265	7	4·350
12·874	8	4·971
14·483	9	5·592
16·093	10	6·214
40·232	25	15·535
80·465	50	31·070
120·696	75	46·605
160·930	100	62·136
321·860	200	124·272
482·790	300	186·408
643·720	400	248·544
804·650	500	310·680

Kilogrammes—pounds

Kg.	Lb. or kg.	Lb.
0·453	1	2·205
0·907	2	4·409
1·360	3	6·614
1·814	4	8·818
2·268	5	11·023
2·721	6	13·228
3·175	7	15·432
3·628	8	17·637
4·082	9	19·841
4·535	10	22·046
9·071	20	44·092
11·339	25	55·116
22·680	50	110·232
45·359	100	220·464

Litres—gallons (imperial)

Litres	Gallons or litres	Gallons
4·55	1	0·22
9·09	2	0·44
13·64	3	0·66
18·18	4	0·88
22·73	5	1·10
27·28	6	1·32
31·82	7	1·54
36·37	8	1·76
40·91	9	1·98
45·46	10	2·20
90·92	20	4·40
136·38	30	6·60
181·84	40	8·80
227·30	50	11·00
340·95	75	16·50
454·59	100	22·00
681·89	150	33·00
909·18	200	44·00

Temperature

Centigrade	Fahrenheit
− 30	− 22
− 20	− 4
− 10	+ 14
− 5	+ 23
0	+ 32
+ 5	+ 41
+ 10	+ 50
+ 20	+ 68
+ 30	+ 86
+ 36·9*	+ 98·4*
+ 40	+104
+ 50	+122
+ 60	+140
+ 70	+157
+ 80	+176
+ 90	+194
+100	+212

* *normal body temperature*

Gradient percentages

%		
10	1 in	10
11	1 in	9·1
12	1 in	8·3
13	1 in	7·7
14	1 in	7·1
15	1 in	6·6
16	1 in	6·2
17	1 in	5·8
18	1 in	5·5
19	1 in	5·3
20	1 in	5
21	1 in	4·7
22	1 in	4·5
23	1 in	4·3
24	1 in	4·1
25	1 in	4
26	1 in	3·8
27	1 in	3·7
28	1 in	3·6
29	1 in	3·4
30	1 in	3·3

Clothing sizes—women

	British	American	French
Dresses	32	10	38
	34	12	40
	36	14	42
	38	16	44
	40	18	46
	42	20	48
Blouses	30	30	42
	32	32	44
	34	34	46
	36	36	48
	38	38	50
	40	40	52
	42	42	54
Sweaters	32	32	42
	34	34	44
	36	36	46
	38	38	48
	40	40	50
Stockings	8	8	0
	$8\frac{1}{2}$	$8\frac{1}{2}$	1
	9	9	2
	$9\frac{1}{2}$	$9\frac{1}{2}$	3
	10	10	4
	$10\frac{1}{2}$	$10\frac{1}{2}$	5
	11	11	6
Shoes	2	$3\frac{1}{2}$/35	34
	$2\frac{1}{2}$	4/40	35
	3	$4\frac{1}{2}$/45	$35\frac{1}{2}$
	$3\frac{1}{2}$	5/50	36
	4	$5\frac{1}{2}$/55	$36\frac{1}{2}$
	$4\frac{1}{2}$	6/60	$37\frac{1}{2}$
	5	$6\frac{1}{2}$/65	38
	$5\frac{1}{2}$	7/70	$38\frac{1}{2}$
	6	$7\frac{1}{2}$/75	$39\frac{1}{4}$
	$6\frac{1}{2}$	8/80	40
	7	$8\frac{1}{2}$/85	$40\frac{1}{2}$
	$7\frac{1}{2}$	9/90	41
	8	$9\frac{1}{2}$/95	42

Clothing sizes—men

	British/American	French
Shirts	13	33
	$13\frac{1}{2}$	34
	14	35–36
	$14\frac{1}{2}$	37
	15	38
	$15\frac{1}{2}$	39
	$15\frac{3}{4}$	40
	16	41
	$16\frac{1}{2}$	42
	17	43
Shoes	7/8	$40\frac{1}{2}$
	8/9	42
	9/10	43
	10/11	44
	11/12	$45\frac{1}{2}$
	12/13	47
	13/14	48

Currency

100 centimes = 1 franc
Sterling. £1.00 = 11.90 francs
United States dollars. $1.00 = 5.00 francs
Notes: 5, 10, 50, 100, 500 francs
Coins: 1, 2, 5, 10, 20, 50 centimes
1, 5, 10 francs

Francs	Sterling	U.S. dollars	Sterling new pence (p)
1	£0·085	$0.20	8½p
2	0·17	0.40	17
3	0·255	0.60	25½
4	0·34	0.80	34
5	0·425	1.00	42½
6	0·51	1.20	51
7	0·595	1.40	59½
8	0·68	1.60	68
9	0·765	1.80	76½
10	0·85	2.00	85
20	1·70	4.00	
30	2·55	6.00	
40	3·40	8.00	
50	4·25	10.00	
60	5·10	12.00	
70	5·95	14.00	
100	8·50	20.00	
200	17·00	40.00	
500	42·50	100.00	
1000	85·00	200.00	

£ in francs	Pounds sterling or U.S. dollars	$ in francs
11·90	1	5.00
23·80	2	10.00
35·70	3	15.00
47·60	4	20.00
59·50	5	25.00
71·40	6	30.00
83·30	7	35.00
95·20	8	40.00
107·10	9	45.00
119·00	10	50.00

Old sterling currency (£ s d)	Sterling decimal currency : new pence (p)	Old sterling currency (£ s d)	Sterling decimal currency : new pence (p)
1d	$\frac{1}{2}$p	5s	25p
2d	1p	6s	30p
3d	1p	7s	35p
4d	$1\frac{1}{2}$p	8s	40p
5d	2p	9s	45p
6d	$2\frac{1}{2}$p	10s	50p
7d	3p	11s	55p
8d	$3\frac{1}{2}$p	12s	60p
9d	4p	13s	65p
10d	4p	14s	70p
11d	$4\frac{1}{2}$p	15s	75p
1s	5p	16s	80p
2s	10p	17s	85p
3s	15p	18s	90p
4s	20p	19s	95p

£1, or 20 old shillings = 100 new pence (p)

Appendix VI

Essential reference books for mountaineering

Appendix VII

French Government Tourist Offices

Selected Climbs in the Mont Blanc Range
2 volumes. Alpine Club, London, 1967

Encyclopaedic Dictionary of Mountaineering
Constable, London, 1968

Mountaineering Handbook
Penguin Books, 1965, 1968

Belgium
25–27 Boulevard Adolphe-Max, Brussels

Britain
178 Piccadilly, London W.1

Canada
1170 Rue Drummond, Montreal

Denmark
12 Amaliegade, Copenhagen

Ireland
10 Arcade Grafton, Dublin

Netherlands
Noordeinde 138, The Hague

South Africa
Suite 632, 6th floor, B.P. Centre, 36 Kerk Street, Johannesburg

Sweden
3 Jakobstorg, Stockholm

United States
610 Fifth Avenue, New York
18 South Michigan Avenue, Chicago
323 Geary Street, San Francisco
9418 Wilshire Boulevard, Beverley Hills, L.A.

Index

Notes